VEGAN FOR THE HOLIDAYS

CELEBRATION FEASTS for THANKSGIVING through NEW YEAR'S DAY

ZEL ALLEN

BOOK PUBLISHING COMPANY

SUMMERTOWN, TENNESSEE

Cover and interior design: Scattaregia Design
Cover and interior photos: Andrew Schmidt, Warren Jefferson
Food styling: Barbara Jefferson, Ron Maxen

Book Publishing Company
PO Box 99
Summertown, TN 38483
888-260-8458
bookpubco.com

ISBN: 978-1-57067-284-2

Printed in the United States of America

18 17 16 15 14 13 12   1 2 3 4 5 6 7 8 9

Library of Congress Cataloging-in-Publication Data

Allen, Zel.
  Vegan for the holidays : celebration feasts for Thanksgiving through New Year's Day / Zel Allen.
      p. cm.
  Includes index.
  ISBN 978-1-57067-284-2 (pbk.) -- ISBN 978-1-57067-926-1 (e-book)
  1. Vegan cooking. 2. Holiday cooking. I. Title.
  TX837.A379 2012
  641.5'636--dc23
                         2012011942

Printed on recycled paper

Book Publishing Company is a member of Green Press Initiative. We chose to print this title on paper with 100% postconsumer recycled content, processed without chlorine, which saved the following natural resources:

- 41 trees
- 1,190 pounds of solid waste
- 18,778 gallons of water
- 4,164 pounds of greenhouse gases
- 17 million BTU of energy

For more information on Green Press Initiative, visit greenpressinitiative.org. Environmental impact estimates were made using the Environmental Defense Fund Paper Calculator edf.org/papercalculator.

Contents

Dedication

*To **Reuben**, who nourishes me
with constant inspiration
and sweet, loving support.*

Acknowledgments

REUBEN, MY LIFE PARTNER, CHEERLEADER, LOVING HUSBAND, and 24/7 supporter team, earns 200 percent of my love and appreciation for having such steadfast faith in my cooking endeavors. He never let me give up when I had a bad day and my Apricot, Date, and Hazelnut Sticky Pie failed for the fourth time in a row. Vegan households across the country may also want to thank Reuben while they feast their eyes on this delicious treat at dessert time.

Chuck, Bruce, Amy, and Gregg, my four fabulous offspring, are always in my heart and earn my loving appreciation for their continued encouragement of my creative efforts.

Great big bear hugs to Amy, who spent three precious days of her vacation to apply her cook's eye reading through the manuscript with me and offering a multitude of creative suggestions.

My faithful recipe testers belong to a very impressive category of human beings dedicated to making this a better vegan world. Because I've incorporated many of their thoughtful suggestions, I felt I had my own staff of kitchen elves. Their efforts have been so invaluable, and I remain indebted to them. Sincere thank-you's to Alberta Knaack, Aoife McGuirk, Arlene Zsilka, Betty Bobu, Bev Hahler, Bianca Phillips, Chris Summers, Midge Constantino, Cyndi Leedy, Tammy Allen, Del Edwards, Nancy DeVries, Fay Kahn, Yvonne Fide, Gina Sengupta, Joanne Mitchell, JJ Loyonnet, Kathi Schilling, Lane Goldman, Leona Minckler, Lenore Skomal, Marilee Collins, Lee Yeager, Mark Cantin, Michael Montroy, Michelle Monteleagre, Patty and Jim Moore, Tom Peacock, Michael Pickel, Doug Watkins, Saul Beaumont, Sue Hansen, Sharon St. James, Stacey Matrazzo, Susan Lasken, Tami Kettle, Ted Lai, and Yael Kisel.

Appreciation goes to Patrice Fisher for helping me present the Kwanzaa introduction with accuracy and inclusiveness and for directing me to a great resource.

When Cynthia and Bob Holzapfel of Book Publishing Company accepted this, my second cookbook, for publication, I was elated and nearly burst with joy. I owe them my deep gratitude for welcoming *Vegan for the Holidays* into the BPC family and showering it with nurturing support.

Over the years I've been co-publishing the Internet magazine *Vegetarians in Paradise* with my husband, I've reviewed numerous vegan books and am keenly aware of the sharp eye and intuitive sense it takes to be a good editor. My cup runneth over with not one, but two exceptional editors. Carol Wiley Lorente, editorial director, took my unpolished manuscript and honed and shaped it into its present shiny, sleek form, while copy editor Terry Christofferson made sure none of the delicious ingredients went astray.

Another leg of the publishing team is Chef Ron Maxen and photographer Warren Jefferson. While Chef Ron prepared and styled the holiday dishes, Warren applied his art with skilled camera work, resulting in brilliant, colorful, and enticing photos. Working with Warren were Barbara Jefferson and Andrew Schmidt. A banquet of thank-you's go to the whole publishing team for its part in bringing *Vegan for the Holidays* to life.

Introduction

WITH AN IDEA SIMMERING IN THE BACK OF MY MIND FOR SOME TIME NOW, I feel this is the right time to bring it to a boil, finish it off, plate it, garnish the platter, and present it at the holiday table. Braising, roasting, and sautéing in my kitchen is an abundant crop of indulgent recipes harvested just for the holidays. While many of us take pleasure in cooking throughout the year, we know the holiday season is that special time when those who seldom cook a meal from scratch will haul out the chopping block, mash some potatoes, and consult the family about vegetable preferences.

These past four years, I've poked a spatula into every nook and cranny of my kitchen, gleaning ideas to infuse plenty of spice into those special festive meals when people come together with friends and family to celebrate the holidays.

My aim is to offer vegan holiday foods that are just as delicious, innovative, and elegant as their hallowed meat-based counterparts. Holiday dishes for the festive vegan table center on fresh foods harvested from nature and prepared from scratch and are far more healthful and lower in saturated fat than traditional fare.

Because my family and I share the holidays with friends and other family members who are not vegan or who may have only rarely tasted festive dishes without animal ingredients, I want to provide celebration foods anyone would be proud to serve. And because the eyes are the first to experience the feast, I unleash the usual boundaries and think extravagantly: A holiday meal doesn't have to cost more; it simply has to look that way. Imagine the praise when serving a lavish-looking dish that makes everyone inhale audibly and exclaim with sounds of delight.

Fresh from the oven to the Thanksgiving table are some delectable, hearty, and innovative entrées, such as the picturesque, voluptuous wild rice, vegetable and nut-filled Thanksgiving Phyllo Pie, along with a lavish feast of cranberry appetizers, side dishes, and even beverages.

For Thanksgiving, I'd originally planned to include a recipe for mashed potatoes, but then I shed that idea because most people already know how to prepare them. Then I had second thoughts and included it with the Thanksgiving side dishes we simply cannot leave behind. To offer a truly memorable stuffing,

I prepared a pot of wild rice, combined it with shiitake mushrooms, pecans, and the perfect balance of seasonings to bring a bountiful bowl of Savory Sourdough and Wild Rice Stuffing to the table.

Dessert is that richly spiced old standby, Williamsburg "Pumpkin" Pie, along with Apples 'n' Cream Pie. Fondly, we can join together to raise cups of silky smooth Pumpkin-Apple Nog to end the meal with a toast.

While some choose to celebrate Christmas with simple, everyday comfort foods, I've adopted the philosophy that celebration foods ought to stand apart from our day-to-day fare. Holidays are distinguished from ordinary days and beg for foods infused with novel touches, such as Pear and Butternut Bisque with Cranberry-Pear Compote. I still bring the leafy greens to the table but with dazzling touches like those featured in the Spinach Salad with Beets and Pomegranates, brazenly decked out in bold Christmas colors and served with a knockout Cranberry-Pomegranate Dressing.

I feel grateful for the rich bounty sown and harvested by our American farmers, who have enabled us to celebrate with an abundance of fresh foods.

Jewish holidays are emphatically centered on food, and Hanukkah is no exception. I couldn't resist stirring up a kettle of Sweet and Sour Cabbage Borscht, a time-honored Eastern European soup that makes a delicious starter. To accompany the traditional Potato Latkes with Tofu Sour Cream and Applesauce, I've included Carrot and Sweet Potato Tzimmes. Another memorable sweet, the Cranberry Apple Strudel, is still the revered, old-fashioned dessert from Eastern Europe made even more irresistible by its twenty-first century makeover.

Kwanzaa, a recently created holiday, honors the ancient roots of the African-American culture and celebrates the weeklong holiday with special rituals and symbolic items. Eventually, each day's special ritual leads everyone to the table for a delicious meal. I hope you'll take part in exploring the traditional African-American foods such as Sweet Potato Pie with Cashew-Ginger Crème, Southern Cornbread, Mustard Greens with Tempeh Bacon, and a host of delicious pumpkin dishes.

Whether I've thrown a New Year's Eve bash with a lavish spread of great-tasting finger foods or welcomed in the new year with an open-house, soup-and-chili party, I always find the guests mingling at the table and sampling everything edible. And if, by chance, they leave the table briefly to chat with a friend, I see them returning to taste one more tidbit of New Year Log in Spicy Pecan Gremolata or dip their spoons into the thick and creamy Sweet Potato Soup.

So, I would like to welcome you to a season of jubilant celebrations, complete with irresistible vegan dishes that reflect the beautiful bounty of harvest foods—the creamy squash and pumpkins, tart cranberries, sweet persimmons, juicy pomegranates, freshly cooked chestnuts, crunchy nuts, earthy wild rice, and the herbs and spices that are inseparable from the season. In the pages of this volume, you'll find a banquet of irresistible heritage dishes—some dating back to earlier centuries—innovatively updated with novel touches.

While my focus has been solely on the foods that grace the holiday table, I'm fully aware the holidays came about to mark meaningful events of historical or religious nature. But, after all the hustle and bustle of party planning, gift shopping, gift wrapping, addressing cards, and attending holiday rituals and ceremonies, it all boils down to gathering with friends and loved ones and enjoying a fabulous meal of simple comfort foods or elegant gourmet creations. Food, after all, is a powerful bonding agent that seals warm memories of cherished occasions.

My hope is to bring grace and elegance to the table and establish new holiday food traditions with a compassionate focus that vegans can enjoy with guilt-free gusto.

As I sit down to plan my own family holiday dinners, I feel grateful for the rich bounty sown and harvested by our American farmers, who have enabled us to celebrate with an abundance of fresh foods. And it gives me deep pleasure to invite you to join me in the kitchen throughout the season, as together we participate in fun celebrations and conclude each event with a darned good meal. And now, let's bring on the holiday feasts!

CHAPTER 1

Thanksgiving
Gone Deliciously Vegan

THANKSGIVING IS THE QUINTESSENTIAL HALLOWED AMERICAN HOLIDAY that plunges us into the season of treasured nostalgic memories and sends us scurrying and planning to celebrate with those we cherish. The holiday also gives us the opportunity to express appreciation for our many blessings.

Thanksgiving arrives with expectations for a day of royal feasting. Friends and family gather at the vegan table to enjoy a jubilant celebration rich with savory, succulent flavors that bathe the taste buds with stunning treats of the harvest. It's the holiday that kindles lasting food memories.

The season begs for dishes infused with aromatic herbs. Sweet potatoes and squash reach new heights with a touch of spice and a hint of tart fruits, such as fresh cranberries or quince. Fragrant herbal bouquets of sage, bay leaves, and marjoram drift from the kitchen, ignite the senses, and invite us to join the festivities at the table.

Thanksgiving desserts are a celebration of spices, such as cinnamon, nutmeg, cloves, and ginger, that join together for the highly anticipated finish to the meal.

The vegan Thanksgiving menu yearns for a few classic signature dishes that have become cherished, annual must-haves for the main course. Those dishes ought to be easy to assemble, look inviting, have wonderful aromas, and deliver captivating flavors. In the many years my family and I have been sharing holiday meals with nonvegetarians, we've witnessed not one person who has remarked about missing the turkey. Quite the contrary, most guests are surprised at the bountiful variety of delicious foods and are delighted with the opportunity to experience a true vegan feast first hand.

Yin-Yang Thanksgiving Pâté

Makes 3 cups; 10 to 12 servings

With a touch of playful sculpture, two tasty appetizer pâtés become one very striking presentation with an underlying philosophical message: a balanced approach to everyday life. Accompany with whole-grain crackers or toasted pita wedges, or spoon into leaves of Belgian endive.

Carrot Pâté

1¼ cups chopped carrots

1¼ cups chopped red bell pepper (about 1 large pepper)

1 cup raw or roasted cashews or macadamias

2 tablespoons plus 1 teaspoon freshly squeezed lemon juice

1½ teaspoons minced peeled fresh ginger

¾ teaspoon salt

¼ teaspoon ground pepper

Pinch cayenne

Mushroom Pâté

1 pound cremini or button mushrooms, coarsely chopped

1 small onion, coarsely chopped

2 large cloves garlic, chopped

¼ cup water

½ cup walnuts

1 tablespoon nutritional yeast flakes

1 teaspoon freshly squeezed lemon juice

1 teaspoon salt

1. To make the carrot pâté, put the carrots, bell pepper, cashews, lemon juice, ginger, salt, pepper, and cayenne in a food processor. Process for 1 minute, or until smooth, stopping occasionally to scrape down the work bowl. Transfer to a small bowl and wash and dry the processor bowl.

2. To make the mushroom pâté, cook and stir the mushrooms, onion, garlic, and water in a large skillet over high heat for 3 or 4 minutes, or until the onion is transparent and the mushrooms are softened. Add 1 or more tablespoons of water as needed to prevent burning. There should be at least 1 tablespoon of liquid remaining in the pan.

3. Transfer the mushroom mixture and remaining liquid into the food processor and add the walnuts, yeast flakes, lemon juice, and salt. Process until smooth, stopping occasionally to scrape down the work bowl.

4. To assemble, remove 1 tablespoon of each pâté and set aside. Spoon the remaining mushroom pâté onto half of a dinner plate. Using the back of a spoon, form half of the yin-yang symbol. (See illustration below.)

5. Spoon the remaining carrot pâté onto the plate and form the other half of the symbol. Place the reserved tablespoon of each pâté into the widest portion of the opposite color. Smooth the edges to form a circle.

Stuffed Tomatoes with Edamame Pâté

Well-seasoned and perked up with chili powder, this tasty pâté tucked into hollowed-out cherry tomatoes makes a delicious and attractive holiday starter.

10 to 15 large cherry tomatoes or small Roma tomatoes

8 ounces edamame, cooked and shelled

2 tablespoons freshly squeezed lemon juice

2 tablespoons tamari

2 tablespoons water

1 tablespoon tahini

1 tablespoon grated peeled fresh ginger

2 cloves garlic

1 teaspoon rice vinegar

¼ teaspoon salt

⅛ teaspoon chipotle chile powder

Pinch cayenne (optional)

Paprika, for garnish

1 cup sliced kalamata olives, for garnish

1. Using a serrated grapefruit or paring knife, cut the top off each tomato. Scoop out the tomato pulp and seeds. If using Roma tomatoes, cut them in half crosswise and scoop out the pulp and seeds. Save the pulp for another purpose. Set the tomatoes aside and prepare the filling.

2. Put the edamame, lemon juice, tamari, water, tahini, ginger, garlic, vinegar, salt, chipotle powder, and optional cayenne in a food processor. Process until smooth and creamy, stopping occasionally to scrape down the work bowl.

3. Fill the tomatoes with the edamame mixture. Sprinkle lightly with paprika and garnish with an olive slice if desired.

Sesame Appetizer Balls

These captivating starters explode with pungent flavor and can be served warm, chilled, or at room temperature.

2 slices whole wheat bread

1 tomato, seeded and coarsely chopped

½ cup coarsely ground walnuts

⅓ cup diced sweet onion

¼ cup minced Spanish olives

2½ tablespoons red wine vinegar

1 to 2 cloves garlic, minced

½ teaspoon salt

½ to ⅔ cup unhulled sesame seeds

¼ bunch parsley, for garnish

3 cherry tomato halves, for garnish

1. Preheat the oven to 375 degrees F. Line a 17½ x 12½-inch rimmed baking sheet with parchment paper.

2. Tear the bread into pieces and put them in a medium bowl. Pour water over the bread to cover. Drain thoroughly, squeeze the bread very dry and put it in a food processor.

3. Add the tomato, walnuts, onion, olives, vinegar, garlic, and salt. Process until ingredients are incorporated and form a coarse mixture, stopping occasionally to scrape down the work bowl.

4. Put the sesame seeds in a small, deep bowl. Roll tablespoonfuls of the bread mixture into 1-inch balls. Roll each ball in the sesame seeds to coat completely.

5. Place the balls on the prepared pan. Bake for 25 to 30 minutes, or until lightly browned. Arrange the parsley around the perimeter of a serving platter and place cherry tomato halves in parsley if desired. Transfer the balls to the serving platter.

Garlicky Chestnut Butter

Consider this buttery spread as a tasty accompaniment to any savory dish, and use as you would a relish.

⅓ **cup chopped onion**

2 **cloves garlic, coarsely chopped**

¼ **teaspoon dried thyme**

½ **cup water**

1¼ **cups cooked and peeled coarsely chopped chestnuts**

¼ **teaspoon salt**

1 **sprig parsley, for garnish**

1. Cook and stir the onion, garlic, thyme, and ¼ cup of the water in a medium skillet over medium-high heat for 3 to 4 minutes, or until the onion has softened. Add 1 or more tablespoons of water as needed to prevent burning.

2. Transfer the mixture to a food processor. Add the chestnuts, salt, and the remaining ¼ cup of water. Process for 1 or 2 minutes, or until smooth and creamy, stopping occasionally to scrape down the work bowl. Transfer to a serving bowl. Garnish with the parsley if desired.

Cranberry-Pear Compote

This recipe combines cranberries with pears, cinnamon, and ginger, and it's a winner. Prepare this a day in advance to give it time to set up in the refrigerator.

1 **(12-ounce) package fresh cranberries**

1 **large firm pear, peeled, cored, and diced**

1 **cup organic sugar**

¾ **cup water**

1 **(3-inch) cinnamon stick**

1 **tablespoon minced peeled fresh ginger**

1 **tablespoon freshly squeezed lemon juice**

Combine all the ingredients in a 3-quart saucepan. Cover and bring to a boil over high heat. Just as the mixture comes to a boil, immediately decrease the heat to low and simmer for 10 to 12 minutes. Let cool completely and refrigerate 8 to 12 hours to thicken.

Curried Kabocha Soup

Lightly spiced with curry, cardamom, and nutmeg, this creamy squash soup brings a golden glow to the holiday table and makes a delicious first course.

1 kabocha squash (2 ½ to 3 pounds)

1 large and 1 medium onion, chopped

2 large carrots, finely diced

½ cup water

2 rounded teaspoons minced peeled fresh ginger

1 ¼ teaspoons curry powder

¾ teaspoon salt

½ teaspoon ground turmeric

¼ teaspoon ground cardamom

¼ teaspoon ground nutmeg

4 cups unsweetened soy milk, rice milk, or nut milk

2 cups vegetable broth

2 teaspoons freshly squeezed lemon juice

2 tablespoons maple syrup (optional)

⅓ cup sweetened dried cranberries, for garnish

1. Preheat the oven to 425 degrees F. Line a 17½ x 12½-inch rimmed baking sheet with parchment paper or aluminum foil.

2. Place the squash on the prepared pan. Bake for 1 hour, or until softened when lightly pressed.

3. Meanwhile, cook and stir the onions, carrots, water, ginger, curry powder, salt, turmeric, cardamom, and nutmeg in an 8- to 10-quart stockpot over high heat for 12 to 15 minutes, or until the vegetables are lightly browned. Remove ⅔ cup of the onion mixture and set aside.

4. Cut the squash in half. Remove and discard the seeds. Scoop the flesh into the stockpot with the onion mixture. Add the soy milk and vegetable broth. Use an immersion blender to process the soup in the stockpot, or put the soup in a blender in batches. Process until smooth and creamy, stopping occasionally to scrape down the blender jar.

5. Return the soup to the stockpot. Cook over medium heat until heated through. Stir in the lemon juice and the optional maple syrup.

6. Ladle the soup into bowls. Spoon some of the reserved onion mixture into the center of each serving. Garnish with a few dried cranberries if desired.

Butternut Squash, Beet, and Apple Soup Makes 8 to 10 cups; 5 to 6 servings

A small cup of this soup makes a tasty starter to a festive meal, while a hearty bowl will satisfy for a light meal during the busy holiday season.   *SEE PHOTO FACING PAGE 26*

**1 butternut squash
(1½ to 2 pounds), peeled**

2 small beets, peeled

3½ cups water

1 large onion, chopped

1 large carrot, diced

2 stalks celery, chopped

1½ cups apple juice

2 apples, peeled, cored, and coarsely shredded

½ teaspoon salt

Garnishes

Pinch ground nutmeg

1½ cups corn kernels

½ cup sweetened dried cranberries

1. Cut the squash and the beets into ½-inch cubes and put them in an 8- to 10-quart stockpot with 3 cups of the water. Cover and bring to a boil over high heat. Decrease the heat to medium and simmer for about 25 minutes, or until the squash and beets are tender.

2. Meanwhile, in a large skillet over medium heat, cook and stir the onion, carrot, celery and the remaining ½ cup water for 12 to 15 minutes, or until the vegetables are very soft and beginning to brown. Add 1 or more tablespoons of water as needed to prevent burning.

3. Add the onion mixture and the apple juice to the stockpot with the squash and the beets. Use an immersion blender to process the soup in the stockpot, or put the soup in a blender in batches. Process until the soup is smooth or slightly chunky, as desired, stopping occasionally to scrape down the blender jar. Return the soup to the stockpot.

4. Add the shredded apples and salt and mix well. Cook the soup until simmering.

5. Ladle the soup into bowls. Garnish each serving with a pinch of nutmeg, 2 tablespoons of corn, and a few dried cranberries if desired.

Lemony Carrot Soup

This radiant, savory carrot soup sparks the appetite with its light texture and aromatic lemon-dill seasonings.

⅔ cup cashews

2 pounds carrots (about 7 large), coarsely shredded

1 large onion, chopped

2 stalks celery, chopped

2 cloves garlic, sliced

2 ½ cups water

4 cups vegetable broth

¾ cup chopped fresh dill weed

1½ teaspoons ground coriander

1 teaspoon salt

¼ teaspoon ground nutmeg

Freshly ground pepper

¼ cup freshly squeezed lemon juice

1. Put the cashews in an electric coffee grinder, food processor, or blender. Process the cashews to a fine powdery meal. (Avoid overprocessing, or it will turn into cashew butter.) Set aside.

2. Cook and stir carrots, onion, celery, garlic, and ½ cup of the water in an 8- to 10-quart stockpot over high or medium-high heat for 12 to 15 minutes, or until the vegetables are softened and beginning to brown. Add 1 or more tablespoons of water as needed to prevent burning.

3. Decrease the heat to medium-high and add the vegetable broth, the remaining 2 cups of water, ½ cup of the dill, coriander, salt, nutmeg, pepper, and the reserved ground cashews to the stockpot and simmer 10 minutes.

4. Use an immersion blender to process the soup in the stockpot, or put the soup in a blender in batches. Process until smooth but slightly textured, stopping occasionally to scrape down the blender jar. Return the soup to the stockpot.

5. Add the lemon juice. Simmer for 1 or 2 minutes, and adjust the seasonings.

6. Ladle the soup into bowls. Garnish each serving with the remaining dill if desired.

Pomegranate-Apple Salad with Ginger and Mint

Makes 6 servings

With each bite of this tasty fruit mélange, pomegranate seeds release their rich, ambrosial juices, delivering sweetness with a pleasing crunch.

1 large pomegranate

2 sweet, crisp apples, unpeeled, chopped

8 ounces edamame, cooked and shelled

1 navel orange, peeled and chopped

3 tablespoons maple syrup

2 tablespoons freshly squeezed lemon juice

2 tablespoons pomegranate molasses

1 tablespoon balsamic vinegar

2 to 3 heaping teaspoons minced peeled fresh ginger

¾ teaspoon salt

1 to 2 tablespoons minced fresh mint leaves

1. Cut the pomegranate into quarters. Carefully remove the seeds with your fingers. Put the seeds in a large bowl.

2. Add the apples, edamame, orange, maple syrup, lemon juice, pomegranate molasses, balsamic vinegar, ginger, and salt and toss well to distribute the ingredients evenly.

3. Add half of the mint leaves and mix well. Garnish the top of the salad with the remaining mint leaves. Serve immediately, or refrigerate. Serve the salad within 2 hours.

Thanksgiving Phyllo Pie

Makes 10 to 12 servings

Stately, delicious, and aromatic, this is the dish that will change the minds of those who snicker at the thought of a vegan Thanksgiving dinner. Prepare the filling a day in advance. SEE PHOTO FACING PAGE 26

Filling

3¾ cups water

¾ cup wild rice

½ cup pearl barley

2½ teaspoons salt

⅓ cup whole almonds, coarsely chopped

⅓ cup walnuts, coarsely chopped

⅓ cup pecans, coarsely chopped

2 small russet potatoes, peeled and cut into bite-sized chunks

8 ounces shiitake mushrooms, stems discarded, chopped

1 large onion, chopped

1 large red bell pepper, chopped

2 large carrots, coarsely shredded

2 stalks celery, diced

5 cloves garlic, minced

1 teaspoon dried sage

¾ teaspoon ground cinnamon

¾ teaspoon ground allspice

½ teaspoon dried thyme

½ teaspoon dried marjoram

½ teaspoon dried rosemary

1. Preheat the oven to 350 degrees F.

2. To make the filling, combine 3½ of the water, rice, barley, and 1¼ teaspoons of the salt in a 3-quart saucepan. Cover and bring to a boil over high heat. Decrease the heat to low and cook for 50 to 60 minutes, or until the rice and barley are tender and all the liquid has been absorbed.

3. Meanwhile, place the almonds, walnuts, and pecans in a single layer on a 17½ x 12½-inch rimmed baking sheet. Bake for 8 to 10 minutes, or until lightly toasted. Immediately pour the nuts onto a plate to cool.

4. Put the potatoes in a 1-quart saucepan with water to cover. Cover and bring to a boil over high heat. Decrease the heat to medium and simmer 5 to 7 minutes, or until the potatoes are tender. Transfer the potatoes to a medium bowl with a slotted spoon and mash them.

5. Cook and stir the mushrooms, onion, bell pepper, carrots, celery, garlic, sage, cinnamon, allspice, thyme, marjoram, rosemary, and the remaining ¼ cup water in a deep, 10 or 12-inch skillet over medium-high heat for 12 to 15 minutes, or until the vegetables are softened and beginning to brown. Add 1 or more tablespoons of water as needed to prevent burning.

6. Add the tomatoes, zucchini, raisins, chickpeas, the remaining 1¼ teaspoons of salt, and pepper to the skillet. Cook another 10 minutes, or until the tomatoes are broken down.

7. Add the rice mixture, toasted nuts, and mashed potatoes to the skillet and mix thoroughly. Adjust the seasonings and set aside.

1 large or 2 medium tomatoes, diced

1 large zucchini, chopped

½ cup golden raisins

1 (15-ounce) can chickpeas, drained and rinsed

Freshly ground pepper

Crust

12 sheets phyllo dough, at room temperature

¼ cup canola oil

Garnishes

Ground cinnamon

1 to 2 tablespoons coarsely ground pistachios

1 tablespoon minced fresh mint or parsley

1 small tomato, cut into a rose

8. To make the crust, place a dish towel horizontally on your workspace. Unroll the phyllo dough and place it on the dish towel. Cover it with another dish towel to prevent the phyllo from drying out. (Each time you remove a phyllo sheet, cover the dough with the dish towel.) Pour the canola oil into a small bowl and place it nearby. Lightly oil a 10-inch ovenproof skillet.

9. Remove one sheet of phyllo from the stack, and place it into the prepared skillet, allowing the ends to drape over the side of the skillet. Gently brush the phyllo with oil, including the portion that drapes over the side. Repeat with eight more sheets of phyllo, draping each of the sheets in a different direction to form a circle around the skillet.

10. Spoon the filling into the phyllo crust, packing it firmly. Lift up the edges of the draped phyllo sheets and place them over the filling. Place the remaining three sheets of phyllo on top of the pie, one at a time, brushing each with the oil. Tuck the ends of the three sheets down into the sides of the skillet. Bake for 50 to 60 minutes, or until the crust is golden.

11. To serve, invert the pie onto a large serving platter or tilt the skillet to slide it onto the platter. Garnish the top with the cinnamon, pistachios, and mint and place the tomato rose in the center if desired. Cut the pie into wedges with a serrated knife and remove each wedge with a pie server.

Pistachio and Sweet Pea Torte with Roasted-Tomato Aïoli

Makes 10 to 12 servings

Deliciously seasoned with flamboyant flavors, captivatingly aromatic, and visually appealing, this unique torte is a first-rate holiday entrée that delivers plenty of pizzazz.

Torte

1½ cups water

½ cup cashews

1 tablespoon plus ¼ teaspoon white vinegar or rice vinegar

2½ cups old-fashioned rolled oats

2 teaspoons baking powder

1¾ teaspoons salt

½ teaspoon baking soda

½ cup plus 3 tablespoons coarsely ground pistachios

2 onions, diced

2 carrots, diced

1 stalk celery, diced

1 red bell pepper, diced

6 cloves garlic, minced

1 (2-inch) piece fresh ginger, peeled and grated

1 teaspoon ground cumin

1 teaspoon ground coriander

1 teaspoon poultry seasoning

1. Cover the base of a 9-inch springform pan with a piece of parchment paper 2 inches larger. Snap the collar back onto the base, and cut away the excess paper with scissors. Lightly oil the sides of the pan, place it on a baking sheet, and set aside.

2. To make the torte, pour 1 cup of the water and the cashews into a blender. Process on high speed until smooth and milky. Transfer to a small bowl, stir in the vinegar and set aside to sour.

3. Combine the oats, baking powder, salt, and baking soda in a large bowl and mix well. Stir in ½ cup of the ground pistachios.

4. Preheat the oven to 375 degrees F. Combine the remaining ½ cup of water, onions, carrots, celery, bell pepper, garlic, ginger, cumin, coriander, poultry seasoning, fennel seeds, oregano, marjoram, turmeric, cayenne, and pepper in a large skillet. Cook and stir over medium-high heat for 10 to 12 minutes, or until the vegetables are softened. Add 1 or more tablespoons of water as needed to prevent burning.

5. Add the cooked vegetables and the rice to the oat mixture and combine well.

6. Put the peas in a food processor. Process until creamy, stopping occasionally to scrape down the work bowl. Add the peas and the soured cashew milk to the vegetable mixture and mix well.

½ **teaspoon fennel seeds, coarsely ground with a mortar and pestle**

½ **teaspoon dried oregano**

½ **teaspoon dried marjoram**

½ **teaspoon ground turmeric**

Pinch cayenne

Freshly ground pepper

3 cups cooked short-grain brown rice

1 pound frozen peas, thawed

1 carrot, shredded, for garnish

3 tablespoons minced fresh parsley, for garnish

Aïoli

1 pound Roma tomatoes, cut in half lengthwise

1 cup water

½ **cup cashews**

2 cloves garlic

1 tablespoon plus 2 teaspoons freshly squeezed lemon juice

¾ **teaspoon salt**

¼ **teaspoon ground smoked paprika or liquid smoke**

7. Spoon the mixture into the prepared springform pan and spread to the edges, packing the mixture firmly. Smooth the top and sprinkle with the remaining 3 tablespoons of pistachios. Bake for 55 to 60 minutes, or until the torte is firm when gently pressed. Let cool at least 30 minutes before serving.

8. To make the aïoli, place the tomatoes on a baking sheet, cut side up, and broil about 3 inches from the heat for 15 to 20 minutes, turning twice while broiling, until completely soft.

9. Meanwhile, put the water, cashews, and garlic in a blender. Process until smooth, stopping occasionally to scrape down the blender jar. Add the broiled tomatoes, lemon juice, salt, and paprika to the cashew mixture. Process until smooth and creamy, stopping occasionally to scrape down the blender jar. Transfer the sauce to a 1-quart saucepan and simmer over medium heat for about 5 minutes.

10. To serve, place the springform pan on a large serving platter. To unmold, run a knife around the edge to loosen the torte. Carefully lift off the collar. Garnish the edge of the platter with the shredded carrot and minced parsley if desired. Cut the torte into wedges and serve with aïoli on the side.

Variation: Substitute Tofu Sour Cream (page 83) for the Roasted-Tomato Aïoli.

Savory Lentil Terrine
with Mushroom-Wine Sauce

Makes 6 to 8 servings

Served on a footed cake plate, this captivating lentil pie steals the spotlight. Topping it off is a dramatic spiral of sweet potato slices.

Terrine

½ cup pearl barley

5 cups water

1¼ teaspoons salt

1 pound button mushrooms, chopped

2 large red onions, diced

1 cup brown lentils

1¼ teaspoons poultry seasoning

1 bay leaf

½ teaspoon dried marjoram

Freshly ground pepper

⅔ cup chopped almonds

2 tablespoons plus 1 teaspoon tamari

1 tablespoon tapioca flour

4 sweet potatoes or yams about
2 inches in diameter, peeled
and thinly sliced

2 oranges, sliced, slices cut in half,
for garnish

Sprigs dill, parsley, cilantro,
or watercress, for garnish

1. Cover the base of a 9-inch springform pan with a piece of parchment paper 2 inches larger. Snap the collar back onto the base, and cut away the excess paper with scissors. Lightly oil the sides of the pan, place it on a baking sheet, and set aside.

2. To make the terrine, combine the barley, 1½ cups of the water, and ½ teaspoon of the salt in a 2-quart saucepan. Cover and bring to a boil over high heat. Decrease the heat to low and simmer for 45 to 50 minutes, or until the barley is tender and all the liquid is absorbed. Transfer the barley to a large bowl.

3. Combine the mushrooms, onions, and 3 tablespoons of water in a large skillet. Cook and stir over high heat for about 10 minutes, or until the onions are very tender. Add 1 or more tablespoons of water as needed to prevent burning. Set aside.

4. Combine the remaining 3½ cups of water, lentils, poultry seasoning, bay leaf, the remaining ¾ teaspoon salt, marjoram, and pepper in a 3-quart saucepan. Bring to a boil over high heat. Decrease the heat to medium and simmer about 25 minutes, or until the lentils are tender and no more than 1 or 2 tablespoons of liquid remain.

5. Add the mushroom mixture and the lentils to the barley. Mix well. Add the almonds, tamari, and tapioca flour. Stir until all ingredients are thoroughly combined. Adjust seasonings and set aside.

6. To assemble the terrine, place a slice of sweet potato in the center of the springform pan. From the center, arrange more slices of sweet potato, overlapping each about half way to form a spiral. Cover the bottom of the pan with the sweet potato slices.

7. Spoon the lentil mixture over the potato slices, pressing with the back of a spoon to pack the mixture firmly. Cover the springform pan with aluminum foil and bake for 40 minutes. Remove the foil and bake another 15 to 20 minutes, or until the top is firm when lightly pressed.

Sauce

8 ounces button or cremini mushrooms, sliced

1¾ cups plus 3 tablespoons water

¼ cup tamari

¼ cup dry red wine

2 tablespoons freshly squeezed lemon or lime juice

3 tablespoons cornstarch

8. To make the sauce, combine the mushrooms, 1¾ cups of the water, tamari, wine, and lemon juice in a 2-quart saucepan, and bring to a boil over high heat. Decrease the heat to medium and simmer for 5 minutes.

9. Combine the cornstarch and the remaining 3 tablespoons of water in a small bowl or cup and stir until smooth. Stir the paste into the simmering sauce a little at a time, stirring constantly for about 1 minute, or until thickened to desired consistency.

10. Let the terrine cool 10 to 15 minutes. To unmold the terrine, run a knife around the edge of the springform pan. Place a large platter over the springform pan and invert it onto the center of the platter. Remove the springform collar and carefully slide the terrine onto a footed cake plate. Garnish the perimeter of the cake plate with the orange slices and herb sprigs if desired. Serve with the Mushroom-Wine Sauce and/or Lemon-Dill Silken Sauce (recipe follows) on the side.

Note: Use different varieties and colors of sweet potatoes and yams for a colorful presentation.

Lemon-Dill Silken Sauce
Makes about 1 cup

1 (12-ounce) box soft silken tofu

1 teaspoon salt

1 teaspoon minced fresh dill weed, or ½ teaspoon dried dill weed

Freshly ground pepper

1 to 3 tablespoons freshly squeezed lemon juice

Put the tofu, salt, dill, and pepper in a blender or food processor. Process for about 1 minute, or until smooth and creamy, stopping occasionally to scrape down the blender jar or work bowl. Season with the lemon juice and process until well blended.

Autumn Vegetable Roast

This earthy dish displays the brilliant colors of the autumn season so beautifully, it could almost become the singular side dish you choose to serve.

2 or 3 zucchini, cut diagonally into ½-inch slices

3 large pattypan squash, each cut into 8 wedges

2 large yellow crookneck squash, cut diagonally into ½-inch slices

2 large onions, each cut into 8 wedges

2 cups fresh, frozen, or canned corn kernels

4 tomatoes, each cut into 8 wedges

2 red bell peppers, cut into 1½-inch squares

1 (15-ounce) can black beans, drained and rinsed

2 tablespoons extra-virgin olive oil

Salt

Freshly ground pepper

1½ teaspoons dried thyme

Garnishes

1 bunch thyme, divided into 3 portions

½ bunch parsley, divided into 3 portions

1 small green onion, sliced

1. Preheat the oven to 375 degrees F.

2. Combine the zucchini, pattypans, crooknecks, onions, corn, tomatoes, bell peppers, and black beans in 1 or 2 large ziplock bags. Add the oil, seal the bag and shake well to distribute the oil. Pour the vegetables onto a 15½ x 10½-inch baking sheet or pan.

3. Sprinkle the vegetables with salt, pepper, and thyme and toss well. Roast, uncovered, for 25 to 30 minutes, stirring about half way through. Roast until the vegetables are fork-tender.

4. Spoon into a large, deep, serving platter. To garnish, pair each portion of thyme with a portion of parsley and place them artfully at the edges of the platter; sprinkle green onion slices over the top if desired.

Harvest Succotash

Succotash is an old-fashioned dish that originated with the Narragansett Indians in Rhode Island. Originally made of corn and lima beans, the dish has evolved into a lovely Thanksgiving standard. SEE PHOTO FACING PAGE 26

Succotash

1 pound frozen lima beans

1 pound frozen edamame, cooked and shelled

1 (15-ounce) can corn kernels, drained, or kernels cut from 2 ears of fresh sweet corn

1 (15-ounce) can kidney beans, drained and rinsed

1 red bell pepper, diced

½ cup sweetened dried cranberries

Sauce

2 cups soy milk or nut milk

2 tablespoons nutritional yeast flakes

1 tablespoon freshly squeezed lemon juice

¾ teaspoon salt

½ teaspoon ground nutmeg

¼ teaspoon ground pepper

1 to 2 tablespoons cornstarch

1 to 2 tablespoons water

1. Prepare the lima beans and edamame according to the package directions, drain off any excess cooking liquid, and put them in a 3-quart casserole.

2. Add the corn, kidney beans, bell pepper, and cranberries and mix well to distribute the vegetables evenly. Set aside and preheat the oven to 325 degrees F.

3. To make the sauce, combine the soy milk, nutritional yeast, lemon juice, salt, nutmeg, and pepper in a 2-quart saucepan. Bring to a boil over medium-high heat. Immediately decrease the heat.

4. Combine the cornstarch and water in a small bowl or cup and stir to form a smooth, runny paste. Whisk the paste into the simmering soy milk a little at a time, stirring constantly for about 1 minute, or until the sauce is slightly thickened. For a thicker sauce, combine another tablespoon each of cornstarch and water, add to the simmering liquid and whisk for about 1 minute until thickened. Adjust the seasonings.

5. Pour the sauce over the succotash, mix well, and bake 20 to 25 minutes or until heated through.

Orange-Ginger Glazed Carrots

Though you've planned plenty of green vegetables for the special Thanksgiving meal, carrots brighten up the buffet table with their perky orange glow. I cut them lengthwise to showcase them, and add a lightly sweetened glaze to embolden their flavor.

2 pounds carrots

1 cup freshly squeezed orange juice

2 tablespoons organic sugar, brown sugar, firmly packed, or maple syrup

1 tablespoon finely grated, peeled fresh ginger

1 tablespoon cornstarch

1 tablespoon water

2 or 3 sprigs parsley, fresh mint, or dill weed, for garnish

1. Preheat the oven to 350 degrees F. Using a sharp knife, cut the carrots into quarters lengthwise. Place the carrots in an 11 x 7-inch baking pan and pour in about one-half inch of water. Cover with aluminum foil and bake for 45 to 60 minutes, or until the carrots are just tender.

2. Meanwhile, pour the orange juice, sugar, and ginger into a large, deep skillet and warm over medium-high heat to dissolve the sugar. Decrease the heat to medium. Combine the cornstarch and water in a small bowl or cup and stir to form a smooth, runny paste. Stir the paste into the simmering orange juice mixture a little at a time, stirring constantly for 1 minute, or until slightly thickened. Turn off the heat and set aside.

3. When the carrots are tender, carefully transfer them to the skillet. Toss them gently for 1 or 2 minutes over medium heat to coat them with the glaze. Spoon into a serving dish and garnish with fresh herbs if desired.

Golden Squash Concerto

Butternut squash is so richly flavored on its own, it needs only a few veggie companions to create a tantalizing side dish.

1 butternut squash (about 2 pounds)

1 red onion, cut in half vertically, then sliced into half-moons

1 red bell pepper, cut into ½-inch pieces

1 green bell pepper, julienned

1½ cups apple juice

1 (1-inch) piece fresh ginger, peeled and minced

1 teaspoon dried sage

2 to 3 tablespoons maple syrup

2 teaspoons tamari

¼ teaspoon maple extract

Pinch ground cinnamon

Salt

Freshly ground pepper

3 sprigs parsley, cilantro, or basil, for garnish

1. Peel the squash with a vegetable peeler. Cut the squash into bite-sized pieces and put them in a large, deep skillet or 6-quart saucepan.

2. Add the onion, bell peppers, apple juice, ginger, and sage and cook over medium-high heat, stirring frequently, for 10 to 12 minutes, or until the squash is fork-tender.

3. Add the maple syrup, tamari, maple extract, and cinnamon and cook for another minute. Season with salt and pepper. Spoon the vegetables into a serving bowl or a large platter, and garnish with the fresh herbs if desired.

Chestnut-Smothered Brussels Sprouts

Makes 12 servings

Brussels sprouts and chestnuts may seem like the ultimate cliché of trendy holiday foods, but not so this tasty version that turns Brussels sprouts haters into devoted converts.

1 pound Brussels sprouts, cut into quarters lengthwise

2 cups diced onions

2 cups diced fresh tomatoes

1 cup diced red bell peppers

2 tablespoons extra-virgin olive oil

24 cooked and peeled chestnuts, diced, or 1 cup chopped nuts

½ teaspoon garlic powder

½ teaspoon onion powder

6 pimiento-stuffed green olives, minced

Salt

Freshly ground pepper

1 green onion, sliced, for garnish

1. Combine the Brussels sprouts, onions, tomatoes, bell peppers, and olive oil in a large, deep skillet. Cook and stir for 4 to 5 minutes over high heat, or until the onions are very soft and the tomatoes begin to break down. Add 1 or more tablespoons of water as needed to prevent burning.

2. Add the chestnuts, garlic powder, onion powder, and olives. Season with salt and pepper. Cook another 1 to 2 minutes to heat through. Spoon into a serving bowl or platter and garnish with the green onion if desired.

Roasted-Butternut Sunset

Makes 8 servings

Butternut is a delicious squash on its own, but interwoven with carrots, beets, fresh cranberries, and a little kitchen magic, it becomes an extraordinary fusion of rich flavors and flaming colors.

**1 large butternut squash
(2½ to 3 pounds), peeled and cut
into ¾-inch pieces**

**3 large carrots, peeled and
thickly sliced**

2 small beets, peeled and diced

¾ cup fresh cranberries

1 tablespoon extra-virgin olive oil

1 teaspoon salt

¾ cup orange or tangerine juice

**¼ cup plus 3 tablespoons
maple syrup**

¼ cup white miso

1 teaspoon orange or tangerine zest

**1 green onion, diagonally sliced,
or 1 tablespoon minced fresh parsley,
for garnish**

1. Preheat the oven to 375 degrees F.

2. Put the squash, carrots, beets, cranberries, olive oil, and salt in a large bowl and toss well to coat the vegetables. Transfer the vegetable mixture to a 17½ x 12½-inch rimmed baking sheet. Bake for 15 minutes.

3. Meanwhile, combine the orange juice, maple syrup, miso, and orange zest in a small bowl and whisk until smooth. Remove the vegetables from the oven and pour the orange juice mixture over them. Bake another 15 to 20 minutes, or until the vegetables are tender. Spoon the vegetables into a serving bowl or platter and garnish with the green onion slices if desired.

Red Cabbage and Apple Stir-Fry

Makes 8 servings

While one or more green vegetables are frequently part of the autumn feast, I like to add a sweet-and-sour dish that contributes a perky pungency and flavor diversity to the offerings.

1 small to medium head red cabbage, shredded

1 large onion, chopped

3 large carrots, shredded

2 Granny Smith apples, chopped

3 cloves garlic, thinly sliced

½ cup water

3 tablespoons balsamic vinegar

3 tablespoons brown sugar, firmly packed

2 tablespoons freshly squeezed lemon juice

1 teaspoon salt

¼ teaspoon ground pepper

Pinch cayenne (optional)

1. Combine the cabbage, onion, carrots, apples, garlic, and water in a large, deep skillet or wok. Cook and stir over high heat 3 to 5 minutes, or until the vegetables are just softened. Add 1 or more tablespoons of water as needed to prevent burning.

2. Add the balsamic vinegar, brown sugar, lemon juice, salt, pepper, and optional cayenne, and cook another minute. Adjust the seasonings, and serve warm, at room temperature, or chilled.

▶

Baked Maple Sweet Potatoes

Makes about 6 servings

This lightly sweetened side dish not only tastes great, but it also dazzles the eye with its rich golden hues. For an even more colorful dish, use different varieties of sweet potatoes or yams. SEE PHOTO FACING PAGE 26

½ cup maple syrup

3 tablespoons minced peeled fresh ginger

1 tablespoon plus 1½ teaspoons freshly squeezed lemon juice

1 to 1¼ teaspoons ground cinnamon

¼ teaspoon salt

3 pounds sweet potatoes or yams or a mixture, peeled and thinly sliced

¼ cup raisins

¼ cup sweetened dried cranberries

¼ bunch parsley, for garnish

5 fresh cranberries, for garnish

1. Preheat the oven to 400 degrees F. Lightly oil a 13 x 9-inch glass baking pan.

2. Combine the maple syrup, ginger, lemon juice, cinnamon, and salt in a large bowl and mix well.

3. Add the sweet potatoes, raisins, and cranberries and toss well to coat the potatoes thoroughly with the maple syrup mixture. Transfer the potatoes to the prepared baking pan and cover with aluminum foil. Bake for 45 to 60 minutes, or until the potatoes are tender.

4. Spoon into a serving bowl. Place the parsley at the edge of the bowl and nestle the fresh cranberries into the parsley if desired.

◄

Opposite page (clockwise from upper left):
Sweet Potato Pie with Cashew-Ginger Crème, p. 106

Mac 'n' Cheese, p. 98

Okra Creole, p. 105

Southern Cornbread, p. 102

Jamaican Jerk Tofu, p. 99

Jamaican Rice and Peas, p. 100

Previous page (clockwise from upper left):
Brussels Sprouts Go Seoul Searching, p. 63

Glazed Beets in Maple-Balsamic Sauce, p. 64

Spinach Salad with Beets and Pomegranates, p. 49

Cranberry-Pomegranate Dressing, p. 50

Garlicky Roasted Cauliflower, p. 65

Mashed Potatoes with
Onion-Chardonnay Gravy

Makes 6 to 8 servings

Thanksgiving just wouldn't be complete without a heaping bowl of creamy mashed potatoes.

Potatoes

2½ pounds russet, red, or white potatoes, scrubbed

½ cup minced onion

3 large cloves garlic, minced

3 to 6 tablespoons potato cooking liquid

2 to 3 tablespoons nutritional yeast flakes

Salt

Freshly ground pepper

Paprika, for garnish

1. Cut potatoes into 1-inch chunks and put them in a 4-quart saucepan. Add the onion and garlic and enough water to cover the vegetables.. Cover and bring to a boil over high heat. Decrease the heat to medium and simmer for about 10 minutes, or until the potatoes are fork-tender.

2. To make the gravy, combine ¼ cup of the water, the onions, carrot, garlic, marjoram, tarragon, and cinnamon in a 4-quart saucepan. Cook and stir over medium-high heat for 15 to 20 minutes, or until the onion and carrot are softened and turn delicately brown. Add 1 or more tablespoons of water as needed to prevent burning.

3. Add 2 cups of the remaining water, the Chardonnay, and tamari and bring to a boil. Decrease the heat to medium and simmer 2 to 3 minutes.

4. Combine the cornstarch with the remaining 3 tablespoons water in a small bowl or cup and stir to form a runny paste. Stir the paste into the simmering gravy, stirring constantly for about 1 minute, until thickened to desired consistency.

5. Pour the gravy into a blender, filling the blender jar only halfway. Process until smooth and creamy. Pour in the remaining gravy and process until smooth. Return the gravy to the saucepan to heat through. Alternatively, use an immersion blender to process the gravy in the saucepan until smooth and creamy. Season with salt and pepper.

Gravy

2¼ cups plus 3 tablespoons water

1 large onion, diced

1 carrot, finely diced

1 clove garlic, crushed

¼ teaspoon dried marjoram

¼ teaspoon dried tarragon

Pinch ground cinnamon

¼ cup Chardonnay

1 tablespoon tamari

3 tablespoons cornstarch

Salt

Freshly ground pepper

6. Use a slotted spoon to transfer the potatoes and onion to a large bowl. Add 3 tablespoons of the cooking liquid, 2 tablespoons of the nutritional yeast, salt, and pepper. Mash the potatoes with an old-fashioned potato masher until the potatoes are creamy and well mixed. Add more of the cooking liquid as needed for creamier potatoes. Season with the remaining 1 tablespoon of nutritional yeast if desired. Avoid overmixing, or the potatoes will become gummy.

7. Spoon the potatoes into a serving bowl and sprinkle lightly with paprika if desired. Serve with gravy on the side.

Savory Sourdough and Wild Rice Stuffing

Makes 8 to 10 servings

Thanksgiving without a succulent stuffing would be unimaginable. Divinely savory and endowed with the distinctive flavor of shiitake mushrooms, this earthy stuffing makes a side dish that's so tasty it practically wears a halo. Although you can use a food processor to grind the pecans, consider purchasing an inexpensive hand-cranked nut mill for a more perfect grind.

2 cups water

⅔ cup wild rice

¾ teaspoon salt

8 cups cubed sourdough bread

⅔ cup pecans

2 cups vegetable broth

3 stalks celery, chopped

1 onion, chopped

½ cup water

12 ounces to 1 pound fresh shiitake mushrooms, stems discarded, caps sliced, or sliced cremini mushrooms

2 tablespoons plus 1 teaspoon nutritional yeast flakes

2 teaspoons poultry seasoning

1¾ teaspoons salt

1¾ teaspoons lemon pepper, or ½ to ¾ teaspoon ground pepper

1. Preheat the oven to 350 degrees F. Lightly oil a 13 x 9-inch baking pan.

2. To make the wild rice, combine the water, wild rice, and salt in a 2-quart saucepan. Cover and bring to a boil over high heat. Decrease the heat to medium-low and simmer for 45 to 55 minutes, or until most of the liquid is absorbed and the rice is tender. Set aside.

3. Meanwhile, place the bread cubes on one 17½ x 12½-inch rimmed baking sheet and the pecans on another. Toast the pecans for 6 to 8 minutes; immediately transfer them to a plate to cool. Bake the bread cubes for 10 to 12 minutes, or until very dry. Transfer the bread to an extra-large bowl and set aside. When the pecans are cool, grind them into a coarse meal in a hand-cranked nut mill or a food processor. Add the ground pecans to the bread cubes.

4. Add the vegetable broth and mix vigorously with a wooden spoon until the bread cubes begin to break down into a meal.

5. Combine the celery, onion and water in a large skillet and cook and stir over medium-high heat for 12 to 15 minutes, or until the onions are soft and translucent. Add 1 or more tablespoons of water as needed to prevent burning.

Garnishes

1 tablespoon minced fresh parsley

Sprigs fresh herbs

½ lemon slice

½ orange slice

6. Add the mushrooms to the celery mixture. Cook about 10 minutes, stirring frequently, or until the mushrooms are very soft.

7. Transfer the mushroom mixture to the bowl with the bread cubes and add the nutritional yeast, poultry seasoning, salt, and lemon pepper and mix well.

8. Add the cooked wild rice, including any liquid remaining in the saucepan, and mix well. Adjust the seasonings.

9. Spoon the stuffing mixture into the prepared baking pan, cover with aluminum foil and bake for 30 to 35 minutes. Garnish with the minced parsley, fresh herbs, and citrus slices if desired.

Savory Chestnut and Fruit Stuffing

This sumptuous stuffing, replete with chestnuts, is so fruity and ravishing, it makes a delicious meal by itself. Enjoy it as a side dish or use it to stuff acorn, butternut, or delicata squash.

2 cups water

⅔ cup pearl barley

1½ teaspoons salt

8 cups whole wheat bread cubes

2½ cups vegetable broth

3 large sweet onions, chopped

3 stalks celery, chopped

2 large apples, cored and chopped

1¼ cups chopped cooked and peeled chestnuts, or pecans, or walnuts

1 cup golden raisins

¾ cup sweetened dried cranberries

¾ cup chopped dried apricots (preferably Turkish)

1 teaspoon ground cinnamon

½ teaspoon ground nutmeg

½ teaspoon ground pepper

2 tablespoons white miso

1. Preheat the oven to 350 degrees F.

2. Combine the water, barley, and ¾ teaspoon of the salt in a 2-quart saucepan. Cover and bring to a boil over high heat. Decrease the heat to low and simmer for 50 to 60 minutes, or until the barley is tender and all the water is absorbed.

3. Meanwhile, place the bread cubes on a 17½ x 12½-inch rimmed baking sheet. Bake for 10 to 12 minutes, or until dry. Transfer the bread cubes to an extra-large bowl.

4. Add the vegetable broth to the bread cubes and mix vigorously with a wooden spoon until the bread cubes are broken down into a coarse meal. Set aside.

5. Combine the onions and celery in a large, deep skillet and add 2 or 3 tablespoons of water. Cook and stir for 10 to 12 minutes, or until the onions are very soft and translucent. Add 1 or more tablespoons of water as needed to cook the vegetables and prevent burning. Transfer the onion mixture to the bowl with the bread cubes.

6. Add the apples, chestnuts, raisins, cranberries, apricots, cinnamon, nutmeg, pepper, and the remaining ¾ teaspoon salt and mix well.

Garnishes

¼ **bunch parsley**

**3 tangerine wedges or
Fuyu persimmon slices**

3 fresh cranberries

7. Thin the miso with about 3 tablespoons of water, add it to the stuffing mixture and combine well to distribute it evenly. Adjust the seasonings.

8. Spoon the stuffing into a 13 x 9-inch baking pan, cover with aluminum foil and bake for 35 minutes. Remove the foil and bake another 15 to 20 minutes, or until a light crust forms on the top.

9. To serve, garnish one corner of the pan with the parsley and artfully nestle the tangerine wedges and cranberries into the parsley if desired.

Holiday-Ready Apple Crisp

A venerable, time-honored dessert as homespun as they come, this old-fashioned apple crisp is spruced up for the holiday with a blush of cranberries and a touch of citrus zest.

Filling

3 large Granny Smith apples, peeled, cored, cut into quarters, and sliced

1¼ cups fresh cranberries

⅓ cup raisins

⅓ cup dried apricots (preferably Turkish), snipped into quarters

½ teaspoon orange or lemon zest (optional)

⅓ to ½ cup organic sugar

¼ cup whole wheat pastry flour

½ teaspoon ground cinnamon

Topping

¾ cup old-fashioned rolled oats

½ cup whole wheat pastry flour

½ cup brown sugar, firmly packed

½ teaspoon ground cinnamon

½ cup vegan margarine

1. Preheat the oven to 350 degrees F.

2. To make the filling, combine the apples, cranberries, raisins, apricots, and optional orange zest in a large bowl and toss together.

3. Combine the sugar, flour, and cinnamon in a medium bowl. Mix well and add to the apple mixture. Mix thoroughly until well combined. Spoon the mixture into an 8-inch-square baking pan.

4. To make the topping, combine the oats, flour, brown sugar, and cinnamon in a medium bowl and mix well. With a pastry blender or your hands, work the vegan margarine into the flour mixture until it is coarse and lumpy.

5. Sprinkle the topping over the apple mixture. Bake uncovered for 50 to 60 minutes, or until the apples are fork-tender. Let cool 15 minutes and serve warm, or let cool completely and refrigerate until ready to serve.

Williamsburg "Pumpkin" Pie

Makes 1 (9-inch) pie; 6 to 8 servings

You can't miss with this recipe that captures the spicy taste and aroma of a traditional, well-seasoned pumpkin pie but features butternut squash instead. The Pilgrims would have really appreciated this treat, especially with a dollop of Satin Whipped Cream as a finishing touch.

1 Oatmeal Crumb Crust (page 36)

¼ cup plus 2 tablespoons arrowroot starch, or ¼ cup plus 1 tablespoon if using canned pumpkin

¼ cup unsweetened soy milk

1 (12.3-ounce) box extra-firm silken tofu, drained

2 cups cooked, mashed butternut squash or canned pumpkin

1¼ cups plus 2 tablespoons organic sugar

2 teaspoons ground cinnamon

½ teaspoon ground nutmeg

½ teaspoon ground allspice

¼ teaspoon ground cloves

¼ teaspoon ground ginger

Pinch salt

Satin Whipped Cream (recipe follows)

1. Preheat the oven to 350 degrees F. Prepare the Oatmeal Crumb Crust.

2. To make the filling, combine the arrowroot and soy milk in a blender. Process on high speed for 1 minute until smooth and slightly thickened, stopping occasionally to scrape down the blender jar. Set aside in the blender to thicken further.

3. Put the tofu, squash, sugar, cinnamon, nutmeg, allspice, cloves, ginger, and salt in a food processor. Process until smooth and creamy, leaving no bits of white tofu visible, stopping occasionally to scrape down the work bowl.

4. Process the arrowroot mixture again and add it to the batter in the food processor. Process until well incorporated, stopping occasionally to scrape down the work bowl.

5. Spoon the filling into the prepared crust. Use the back of the spoon to spread the filling to the edges and smooth the top.

6. Bake the pie in the middle of the oven for 45 to 50 minutes. The center of the pie will still be slightly soft but will firm when chilled. Let cool completely.

7. Cover and refrigerate for 8 to 12 hours. Serve with Satin Whipped Cream.

Satin Whipped Cream

½ cup cashews

1 cup water

1 small banana

6 tablespoons powdered sugar

½ teaspoon xanthan gum

¼ to ½ teaspoon vanilla extract

1. Put the cashews in a food processor. Process until ground into a fine meal. Transfer to a blender. Put the water, banana, sugar, xanthan gum, and vanilla extract in the blender with the cashew meal. Process for 1 to 2 minutes, or until the mixture becomes thick, smooth and creamy, stopping occasionally to scrape down the blender jar.

2. Transfer the mixture to a covered container and chill for 8 to 12 hours to firm. Covered tightly and stored in the refrigerator, Satin Whipped Cream will keep for about 4 days. Before serving, fluff the mixture with a gentle stir.

Oatmeal Crumb Crust

3 cups old-fashioned rolled oats

¾ cup walnuts

4½ tablespoons canola oil

3 tablespoons organic sugar

3 tablespoons maple syrup

1½ tablespoons freshly squeezed lemon juice

¾ teaspoon salt

1. Pour the oats into a food processor. Pulse 12 to 15 times. Add the walnuts, oil, sugar, syrup, lemon juice, and salt. Process until the mixture is a fine, crumbly meal and holds together when pinched, stopping occasionally to scrape down the work bowl. If needed, add 1 tablespoon of water to help it hold together.

2. Spoon the mixture into a 9 or 10-inch pie pan and press it firmly and evenly into the bottom and up the sides of the pan with your fingers. Press on the edges to firm.

Easy Pumpkin Tofu Cheesecake

Makes 10 to 12 servings

The cheesecake needs several hours to cool and firm in the refrigerator and works best when prepared a day in advance.

1 Flaxseed Pie Crust (page 40)

1 (15-ounce) can pumpkin

1 (14-ounce) package
firm tofu, drained

1 cup plus 2 tablespoons
organic sugar

¼ cup arrowroot starch

2 teaspoons ground cinnamon

1 or 2 teaspoons freshly
squeezed lemon juice

1 teaspoon vanilla extract

¾ teaspoon ground nutmeg

½ teaspoon ground allspice

⅛ teaspoon ground cloves

Pinch salt

Satin Whipped Cream (page 36)

1. Preheat the oven to 350 degrees F. Prepare the pie crust.

2. Put the pumpkin, tofu, sugar, arrowroot, cinnamon, lemon juice, vanilla extract, nutmeg, allspice, cloves, and salt in a food processor. Process until thoroughly blended, thick and creamy, stopping occasionally to scrape down the work bowl. Spoon the filling into the prepared crust and smooth the top and edges.

3. Bake for 55 to 60 minutes, or until the top is firm when lightly pressed. Let cool completely. Cover and refrigerate for 8 to 12 hours.

4. To serve, place the springform pan on a serving platter or footed cake plate. Run a knife around the edge to loosen the cheesecake. Carefully lift off the collar. Cut into wedges and serve with Satin Whipped Cream on the side.

Apples 'n' Cream Pie

Traditions such as old-fashioned apple pie nurture our comfort zones. Give the pie a cool twist and it becomes indulgent, decadent, and ultra celebratory.

1 Oatmeal Crumb Crust (page 36)

Filling

5 or 6 tart apples, peeled, cored, cut into quarters, and thinly sliced

¼ cup plus 2 tablespoons organic sugar

¼ cup raisins

2 teaspoons freshly squeezed lemon juice

2 tablespoons water

½ teaspoon plus ⅛ teaspoon ground cinnamon

1. Preheat the oven to 350 degrees F. Prepare the Oatmeal Crumb Crust.

2. To make the filling, combine the apples, ¼ cup of the sugar, raisins, lemon juice, water, and ½ teaspoon of the cinnamon in a 2-quart saucepan. Cover and bring to a boil over high heat. Decrease the heat to low and cook for 10 minutes. Let the apples cool. Drain liquid.

3. Add the remaining 2 tablespoons of sugar and remaining ⅛ teaspoon of cinnamon and mix well. Spoon into the prepared pie crust.

Topping

2 (12.3-ounce) boxes extra-firm silken tofu

¼ cup organic sugar

¼ cup maple syrup

1 tablespoon plus 1 teaspoon vanilla extract

¼ teaspoon ground cinnamon

⅛ teaspoon ground allspice

⅛ teaspoon ground nutmeg, plus more to sprinkle on top

⅛ teaspoon salt

⅓ cup lightly toasted unsweetened shredded dried coconut, coarsely ground walnuts, or toasted sliced almonds, for garnish

4. To make the topping, put the tofu, sugar, maple syrup, vanilla extract, cinnamon, allspice, nutmeg, and salt in a food processor. Process until smooth and creamy, stopping occasionally to scrape down the work bowl. Spoon the topping over the apple filling, spreading to within 1 inch of the crust. Sprinkle with nutmeg.

5. Bake for 30 minutes. Let cool completely and refrigerate for 8 to 12 hours. Before serving, sprinkle with coconut or nuts if desired.

Flaxseed Pie Crust

You'll welcome this no-fail pie crust into your recipe repertoire because it requires no high-tech culinary skills—only your fingers to press it into the pie pan.

½ cup almonds

1½ cups whole wheat pastry flour

½ cup ground flaxseeds

2 tablespoons brown sugar, firmly packed

½ teaspoon salt

¾ cup water

⅓ cup canola oil

1. Cover the base of a 9-inch springform pan with a piece of parchment paper 2 inches larger. Snap the collar back onto the base, and cut away the excess paper with scissors. Lightly oil the sides of the pan, place it on a baking sheet, and set aside.

2. Put the almonds in a food processor. Process until they form a coarse meal. Add the flour, ground flaxseeds, brown sugar, and salt and process until thoroughly mixed. Add the water and canola oil and process until the mixture becomes a moist, soft dough, stopping occasionally to scrape down the work bowl.

3. Spoon the crust mixture into the prepared pan and use your fingers to press it firmly into the bottom and 1 inch up the side of the pan.

Pumpkin-Apple Nog

This indulgently thick and creamy nog tends to thicken as it stands but is easily thinned with the addition of small amounts of apple juice.

SEE PHOTO FACING PAGE 26

1¼ cups apple juice

1 cup canned or fresh pumpkin

1 cup soy milk, nut milk, or rice milk

½ cup maple syrup

¾ teaspoon plus ⅛ teaspoon ground cinnamon

¼ teaspoon ground nutmeg, plus extra for garnish

Pinch salt

1. Put all the ingredients in a blender. Process until smooth and creamy, stopping occasionally to scrape down the blender jar. Refrigerate the nog until well chilled.

2. To serve, blend the nog briefly to lighten and fluff the mixture. Pour into old-fashioned glasses or punch cups. Sprinkle lightly with nutmeg if desired.

Note: If you wish to add spirits, either brandy or rum makes an excellent choice.

CHAPTER 2

Christmas Spirit
Is in the Air

AS I WAS THINKING AHEAD TO CHRISTMAS, I could almost see the brilliant colors, hear the joyful sounds, and whiff the spicy aromas that entwine the holiday. Christmas, I thought, more than any other holiday of the year, is bigger and grander in every way. Friends, family, and neighbors talk of almost nothing but decorating the Christmas tree, wrapping presents, baking holiday cookies, and squeezing in enough time to buy all the gifts on the Christmas list. Each year as Thanksgiving passes, the excitement and anticipation of Christmas totally envelops me.

Christmas is that time of year that allows us all to express joy in so many ways, especially the joy of sharing so much with those we treasure.

Some of my favorite joys of the season include inviting friends for dinner and treating them to mouth-watering dishes. Seeing the big smiles on friends' faces and hearing their sounds of pleasure with the first bite is my ultimate reward. Food has a sweet way of bringing people together like nothing else can.

Nonvegetarians dining at my table are always amazed at the copious array of foods, the savory flavors, and the lavish presentation, all brought together in a delicious vegan meal. And I see they cannot help but catch the spirit of a luxurious vegan celebration.

Tijuana Tofu Cocktail

Makes 6 to 8 servings

Colorful and inviting, this zesty appetizer comes alive with bright colors, bold flavors, and a glamorous presentation. Serve it in long-stemmed wine glasses or champagne flutes.

1 (14.5-ounce) can diced tomatoes

1½ cups chopped fresh tomatoes

1½ cups diced firm tofu,
or chopped cooked and
peeled chestnuts

1 large avocado, diced

¾ cup chopped onion

⅓ cup chopped cilantro

3 tablespoons freshly squeezed
lemon juice

½ to 1 jalapeño chile, seeded
and minced

½ teaspoon ground cumin

½ teaspoon ground coriander

¼ teaspoon salt

Cilantro sprigs, for garnish

Lime wedges, for garnish

1. Combine the canned and fresh tomatoes, tofu, avocado, onion, cilantro, lemon juice, jalapeño, cumin, coriander, and salt in a large bowl and mix well.

2. To serve, spoon the cocktail into long-stemmed wine glasses, old-fashioned glasses, or glass dessert bowls and garnish each with a sprig of cilantro and a wedge of fresh lime if desired. Serve with spoons. If desired, refrigerate and serve later.

Jolly Green Christmas Tree

Makes 6 to 8 servings

Here's a holiday appetizer that puts yuletide spirit on a plate and unveils your hidden talent as a sculptor. Make it mildly spiced or crank it up to muy picante with extra jalapeño chiles and a pinch of cayenne.

Dip

1 pound frozen peas, thawed

1 (15-ounce) can cannellini or Great Northern beans, drained and rinsed

½ cup coarsely chopped fresh mint leaves

2 tablespoons organic sugar

2 tablespoons freshly squeezed lime juice

½ to 1 jalapeño chile, seeded and coarsely chopped

1 teaspoon salt

¾ teaspoon chipotle chili powder

½ teaspoon garlic powder

½ teaspoon onion powder

¼ teaspoon chili powder

Pinch cayenne (optional)

Ornaments

¼ red bell pepper, finely diced

½ carrot, finely diced

1 green onion, white part only, sliced (optional)

1 whole star anise, or 6 whole cloves

1. Put the dip ingredients in a food processor. Process until smooth and creamy, stopping occasionally to scrape down the work bowl.

2. Spoon the mixture onto a large platter and use the back of a spoon to form the mixture into the shape of a large Christmas tree. Decorate the tree with the bell pepper, carrot, and the optional green onion. Place the star anise at the top or arrange the cloves into a radiating star. Serve with baked tortilla chips, bean chips, toasted pita wedges, or your favorite crackers.

Almond and Olive-Stuffed Brussels Sprouts

Makes 8 to 10 servings

After watching dinner guests take a pass when plain, steamed Brussels sprouts came to the table, I became aware they are not on everyone's list of favorite vegetables. But when I stuffed them and served them as an appetizer, they proved their mojo.

20 fresh Brussels sprouts

½ cup almonds, coarsely chopped

1 (13.75-ounce) can water-packed artichoke hearts, drained

20 pitted kalamata olives, chopped

10 jumbo pimiento-stuffed green olives, chopped

1 shallot, chopped

2 cloves garlic, minced

1. Fill a 4-quart saucepan two-thirds full with water. Cover and bring to a boil over high heat. Meanwhile, trim the Brussels sprouts stems and discard. Cut the sprouts in half lengthwise. Plunge the sprout halves into the boiling water in batches and boil for 1½ minutes, or until they are just tender but still hold their shape. Use a slotted spoon to transfer them to a plate lined with paper towels and repeat the process until all the sprouts are tender.

2. Using a serrated grapefruit or paring knife, carefully scoop out the centers of the sprouts to create a cavity. Reserve the centers for another recipe.

3. To make the stuffing, put the almonds in a food processor. Process until they form a coarse meal, stopping occasionally to scrape down the work bowl. Transfer to a large bowl.

4. Put the artichoke hearts in the food processor. Process until they are coarsely chopped. Add them to the bowl with the almond meal.

5. Put the olives, shallot, and garlic in the food processor. Process briefly, just until chunky. Add the olive mixture to the bowl with the artichokes and almonds. Mix well. If the stuffing seems too dry, add 1 to 3 teaspoons of water to moisten.

½ to ¾ cup **Homemade Parmesan (page 114) or prepared vegan Parmesan**

6 cherry tomatoes, cut into quarters, for garnish

6. Spoon a heaping teaspoon of the stuffing into the cavity of each sprout half. Sprinkle with the Homemade Parmesan and garnish each with a cherry tomato quarter if desired. Serve at room temperature or cover with plastic wrap and refrigerate.

7. To serve warm, preheat the oven to 350 degrees F. Line a 17½ x 12½-inch rimmed baking sheet with parchment paper. Place the stuffed sprouts on the prepared pan. Bake for 10 to 12 minutes or just until heated through. Garnish each with a cherry tomato quarter if desired. Transfer to a serving platter.

Tangy Cranberry Soup

Is it possible that a bowl of cranberry soup can remind you of sweet-and-sour cabbage borscht? This delightful soup has all those robust, pungent flavors and not a shred of cabbage.

2 cups fresh cranberries

4 cups water

**3 cups chopped tomatoes, or
1 (28-ounce) can diced tomatoes**

1 onion, chopped

**¼ cup plus 2 tablespoons
organic sugar**

3 tablespoons Dijon mustard

1 tablespoon rice vinegar

1¼ teaspoons salt

Pinch cayenne

Freshly ground pepper

**1 (15-ounce) can cannellini beans,
drained and rinsed**

1½ cups Tofu Sour Cream (page 83)

1. Put the cranberries, water, tomatoes, onion, sugar, mustard, vinegar, salt, cayenne, and pepper in an 8- to 10-quart stockpot. Cover and bring to a boil over high heat. Decrease the heat to medium-low and simmer for 20 to 25 minutes.

2. Add the beans and simmer another 1 to 2 minutes. Ladle the soup into bowls and swirl a dollop of Tofu Sour Cream into each serving.

Pear and Butternut Bisque
with Cranberry-Pear Compote

Makes about 12 cups; 6 to 8 servings

Passionate about sharing the stunning fruits and vegetables of autumn and winter, I created this silky smooth butternut soup that also expresses my affinity for cranberries and ginger.

1 large onion, chopped

1 stalk celery, chopped

3½ cups water

2 tablespoons minced peeled fresh ginger

¼ teaspoon ground cinnamon

¼ teaspoon ground nutmeg

1 butternut squash (about 2 pounds), peeled and cut into 1-inch chunks

4 Bartlett, Anjou, or Bosc pears, peeled, cored, and cut into 1-inch chunks

1 teaspoon salt

2½ cups Cranberry-Pear Compote (page 9)

1. Combine the onion, celery, ½ cup of the water, ginger, cinnamon, and nutmeg in an 8- to 10-quart stockpot. Cook and stir over high or medium-high heat for 12 to 15 minutes, or until the onion has softened and is beginning to brown. Add 1 or more tablespoons of water as needed to cook the onions and prevent burning.

2. Add the squash and pears and the remaining 3 cups of the water to the stockpot.

3. Cover the stockpot and bring to a boil over high heat. Decrease the heat to medium and simmer for about 15 minutes, or until the squash and pears are very soft.

4. Use an immersion blender to process the soup in the stockpot until smooth and creamy, or put the soup in a blender in batches. Process until smooth and creamy, stopping occasionally to scrape down the blender jar. Return the soup to the stockpot and add the salt.

5. Ladle the soup into bowls and place a heaping tablespoon of chilled Cranberry-Pear Compote into each serving. Swirl the soup lightly and serve.

Winter Almond Chowder

Makes about 16 cups; 12 servings

Within an hour, you'll be brandishing your soupspoon and ravishing a big steaming bowl of delicious chowder.

1½ cups almonds

10 cups water

5 carrots, sliced

3 stalks celery, sliced

1 large onion, chopped

⅓ cup minced fresh parsley

5 cloves garlic, minced

4 cups chopped broccoli

1 (15-ounce) can white kidney beans, drained and rinsed

¼ cup freshly squeezed lemon juice

Pinch cayenne

Salt

Freshly ground pepper

2 green onions, thinly sliced, for garnish

1. Preheat the oven to 350 degrees F. Pour the almonds into a heavy-duty ziplock bag, place the bag on a cutting board, and use a hammer to break them into pieces. Transfer the almond pieces to a 17½ x 12½-inch rimmed baking sheet and toast them for 8 minutes. Immediately transfer them to a plate to cool. When the almonds are cool, put them in a food processor. Process until finely chopped.

2. Combine 8 cups of the water, carrots, celery, onion, parsley, and garlic in a large 8- to 10-quart stockpot. Cover and bring to a boil over high heat. Decrease the heat to medium and simmer for about 20 minutes, or until the carrots begin to soften.

3. Add the broccoli and beans and simmer another 10 minutes. Add the remaining 2 cups of water, lemon juice, and the roasted almonds. Mix well and simmer another 5 minutes to develop the flavors.

4. Season the soup with cayenne, salt, and pepper and garnish with a sprinkle of green onions if desired.

Spinach Salad with Beets and Pomegranates

Makes 4 to 5 servings

With only five ingredients layered to create dramatic color contrast, this stunning salad is one you can proudly show off at the holiday table.

SEE PHOTO BETWEEN PAGES 26–27

1 (8-ounce) package baby spinach

5 beets, peeled, cubed, and cooked, or 1 or 2 (15-ounce) cans diced beets, drained

2 carrots, coarsely shredded

2 large pomegranates

¼ red onion, cut in half vertically, then sliced into half moons

2 cups Maple-Dijon Salad Dressing (recipe follows) or 2 cups Cranberry-Pomegranate Dressing (page 50)

1. Place the spinach in a large, wide salad bowl and heap the beets into the center. Sprinkle the shredded carrots in a ring surrounding the beets.

2. Cut the pomegranates into quarters. Carefully remove the seeds with your fingers. Form a 2-inch ring of pomegranate seeds next to the carrots, leaving a generous border of spinach at the outer edge.

3. Finish with a sprinkle of onions around the outer edge. Bring the salad to the table to show it off. Toss it thoroughly with your choice of dressing before serving.

Maple-Dijon Salad Dressing

Makes 2 cups

This is my vegan, oil-free counterpart to the standard honey-mustard salad dressing.

1 cup water

¼ cup freshly squeezed lemon juice

¼ cup maple syrup

3 tablespoons Dijon mustard

2 tablespoons rice vinegar

½ teaspoon salt

¼ teaspoon ground pepper

¼ plus ⅛ teaspoon xanthan gum or guar gum

1. Put all the ingredients in a blender. Process on high speed for 1½ minutes to allow the xanthan gum to lightly thicken the dressing, stopping occasionally to scrape down the blender jar.

2. Using a funnel, pour the dressing into a narrow-neck bottle for easy serving. Shake well before using. Covered tightly and refrigerated, Maple-Dijon Salad Dressing will keep for 2 weeks.

Cranberry-Pomegranate Dressing

Makes 2 cups

Cranberries and pomegranates lavish a tasty balance of tangy sweetness on any plate of greens.

SEE PHOTO BETWEEN PAGES 26–27

1 cup fresh cranberries

¾ cup water

¼ cup freshly squeezed lemon juice

¼ cup cider vinegar

3 tablespoons pomegranate molasses

1 tablespoon maple syrup

½ teaspoon salt

¼ plus ⅛ teaspoon xanthan gum or guar gum

¼ teaspoon ground pepper

1. Put all the ingredients in a blender. Process on low speed for a few seconds. Increase speed to high and process for 1 minute, to allow the xanthan gum to lightly thicken the dressing, stopping occasionally to scrape down the blender jar.

2. Using a funnel, pour the dressing into a narrow-neck bottle for easy serving. Shake well before using. Covered tightly and refrigerated, Cranberry-Pomegranate Dressing will keep for 1 week.

Tahini-Dijon Salad Dressing

Makes 2 cups

Oil-free, thick, creamy, and ultra savory, this dressing is vibrant on any salad, particularly on dark leafy greens, because it totally tempers their bitter bite.

1¼ cups water

½ cup plus 1 tablespoon tahini

2 tablespoons plus 1 teaspoon tamari

2 tablespoons rice vinegar

1 tablespoon Dijon mustard

1 teaspoon salt

1 teaspoon maple syrup

¼ teaspoon ground pepper

⅛ to ¼ teaspoon xanthan gum or guar gum

1. Put all the ingredients in a blender. Process for 1 minute, or until smooth and creamy, stopping occasionally to scrape down the blender jar. Using a funnel, pour the dressing into a narrow-neck bottle for easy serving.

2. Shake well before using. Covered tightly and refrigerated, Tahini-Dijon Salad Dressing will keep 1 week.

Upbeet Chestnutty Potato Salad

Makes 6 servings

What makes this dish a delightful departure from standard potato salad is the medley of sweet potatoes, chestnuts, and beets laced with a tart touch of lemon juice and vinegar.

4 white or red rose potatoes, peeled and cut into bite-sized chunks

2 large sweet potatoes or yams, peeled and cut into bite-sized chunks

2 large beets, peeled and cut into bite-sized chunks

1 cup cooked and peeled chestnuts, cut into quarters, or lightly steamed sliced carrots

4 green onions, sliced

3 tablespoons extra-virgin olive oil

3 tablespoons seasoned rice vinegar

1 tablespoon freshly squeezed lemon juice

1 teaspoon salt

Freshly ground pepper

Few sprigs herbs, for garnish

1. Put the potatoes, sweet potatoes, and beets in separate saucepans and add enough water to cover them. Cover and bring to a boil over high heat. Decrease the heat to medium-high and cook until the potatoes and beets are just tender when pierced with a fork. The potatoes will cook in 5 to 7 minutes. The beets will take about 25 to 35 minutes.

2. Use a slotted spoon to transfer the potatoes to a large bowl. Line a plate with three layers of paper towels and transfer the beets to the plate. Use extra paper towels to pat the beets dry if necessary.

3. Add the beets, chestnuts, green onions, oil, vinegar, lemon juice, salt, and pepper to the potatoes and toss well. Transfer the salad to a serving dish and garnish with a few sprigs of herbs if desired.

Pistachio-Edamame Salad

You can count on this dish to provide a hearty lunch or light dinner when served with whole-grain bread and a spinach or romaine salad.

2 large Fuyu persimmons, diced

**1 pound edamame,
cooked and shelled**

**1 navel orange, or 2 tangerines,
peeled and chopped**

1 cup minced fresh parsley

6 green onions, sliced

½ cup pistachios, raw or toasted

⅓ cup minced fresh mint leaves

⅓ cup diced red onion

**3 tablespoons freshly squeezed
lemon juice**

1 clove garlic, minced

¾ teaspoon salt

½ teaspoon orange zest

½ teaspoon tamari

¼ bunch parsley, for garnish

**1 whole radish or radish rose,
for garnish**

1. Put half of the persimmons in a large bowl and set aside the remainder for garnish. Add the edamame, orange, parsley, green onions, pistachios, mint, red onion, lemon juice, garlic, salt, orange zest, and tamari and mix well. Adjust the seasonings and transfer the salad to a serving bowl.

2. To garnish, sprinkle the reserved diced persimmons around the outer edge. Place the parsley in the center or at the edge of the salad and nestle the radish in the parsley if desired.

Santa's Swanky Salad

I'll bet Santa would love to sink his fork into this unique salad that brings together a trio of veggies he rarely encounters at the North Pole.

1 bunch watercress, chopped

½ head romaine, chopped

½ bunch mustard greens, chopped

5 beet greens, chopped

½ bunch radishes, sliced

2 stalks celery, sliced

1 large carrot, sliced

1 pound cremini or button mushrooms, sliced

8 ounces shiitake mushrooms, stems discarded, caps sliced

3 tablespoons water

1 tablespoon tamari

1 tablespoon freshly squeezed lemon juice

3 Fuyu persimmons, cut into quarters and sliced, or 3 tangerines, chopped

3 small beets, peeled and shredded

2 tomatoes, cut into 6 wedges each

2 cups Tahini-Dijon Salad Dressing (page 50)

1. Combine the watercress, romaine, mustard greens, beet greens, radishes, celery, and carrot in a large, wide salad bowl and toss well. Set aside.

2. Combine the mushrooms, water, tamari, and lemon juice in a large, deep skillet. Cook and stir over high heat for 2 or 3 minutes, or until the mushrooms are softened. Add 1 or more tablespoons of water as needed to prevent burning.

3. Place the cooked mushrooms into the center of the greens, piling them high. Place 3 clusters of the persimmon slices around the mushrooms and 3 clusters of the shredded beets in the spaces between. Arrange the tomatoes around the perimeter. Toss the salad at the table and serve with Tahini-Dijon Salad Dressing on the side.

Tomato-Pine Nut Pie
with Sweet Potato and Nut Crust

Makes 1 (9-inch) pie; 6 servings

Melt-in-the-mouth delicious and decked out for the festivities, this attractive Italian-inspired dish makes an ideal savory dinner pie with a unique crust.

Crust

12 ounces sweet potatoes or yams, peeled and cut into 1-inch pieces

1¼ cups whole almonds

⅔ cup mashed firm tofu

¼ teaspoon salt

1. Preheat the oven to 350 degrees F. Lightly oil a 9-inch pie pan.

2. To make the crust, put the sweet potatoes in a 2-quart saucepan with water to cover. Cover and bring to a boil over high heat. Decrease the heat to medium and simmer for 5 minutes, or until the sweet potatoes are fork-tender. Drain the sweet potatoes well, transfer them to a large bowl and mash them well. Set aside.

3. Put the almonds in a food processor. Process until they are finely ground yet still retain a little texture. Add the tofu and salt and process until well incorporated, stopping occasionally to scrape down the work bowl. Spoon the tofu mixture into the bowl with the sweet potatoes and mix well.

4. Spoon the sweet potato mixture into the prepared pan. Use your fingers to press it onto the bottom and up the sides of the pan. Build up the sides of the crust ½ inch higher than the pie pan. Bake the crust for 15 minutes and let cool.

Filling

2 green onions, sliced

1 to 2 large cloves garlic, minced

⅓ cup pine nuts

2 to 3 tablespoons Homemade Parmesan (page 114) or prepared vegan Parmesan

2 to 3 tablespoons cornstarch

Salt

Freshly ground pepper

1 small eggplant, peeled and sliced into ⅛-inch slices

4 to 5 large red or green tomatoes, seeded and sliced

5. To make the filling, put the green onions, garlic, pine nuts, and Homemade Parmesan in individual bowls. Sprinkle the cornstarch on a plate.

6. Cover the bottom of the crust with one layer of eggplant slices. (This prevents the crust from getting soggy). Reserve remaining eggplant for another use. Sprinkle the eggplant slices with salt and pepper.

7. Dredge one-third of the slices in the cornstarch. Arrange the dredged tomato slices over the eggplant, filling all the spaces with small bits of tomato. Sprinkle lightly with salt and pepper. Sprinkle one third each of the green onions, garlic, pine nuts, and Homemade Parmesan over the tomatoes. Repeat the process to make three layers.

8. Bake for 45 minutes. Let cool 10 to 15 minutes before serving.

Note: If using green tomatoes, the pie might have to bake another 15 minutes.

Shiitake Tornadoes
in Cashew-Cream Sauce

Makes 12 balls; 8 to 12 servings

This sumptuous yuletide dish makes a showy presentation on the holiday table.

Tornadoes

8 ounces shiitake mushrooms, stems discarded, caps cut into quarters

1 onion, chopped

1 tablespoon tamari

1½ teaspoons dried tarragon

¾ cup water

½ cup pitted kalamata olives

3 cups cooked short-grain brown rice

1 cup old-fashioned rolled oats

½ cup walnuts, coarsely ground

¼ teaspoon salt

Freshly ground pepper

1 cup black or regular sesame seeds

12 long sprigs fresh rosemary, for garnish

6 cherry tomatoes, cut in half, for garnish

1. To make the tornadoes, preheat the oven to 350 degrees F. Line a 17½ x 12½-inch rimmed baking sheet with parchment paper and set aside.

2. Combine the mushrooms, onion, tamari, and tarragon in a large, deep skillet. Add water and cook and stir over medium-high heat for 10 to 12 minutes, or until the mushrooms are cooked and the onion is softened and transparent. Add 1 or more tablespoons of water as needed to prevent burning.

3. Transfer the mushroom mixture to a food processor and add the olives. Process until smooth and creamy, stopping occasionally to scrape down the work bowl. Spoon the mixture into a large bowl.

4. Add the rice, oats, walnuts, salt, and pepper and mix well. Pour the black sesame seeds into a deep, medium bowl.

5. Using your hands, form the mushroom mixture into balls about 1½ inches in diameter. Roll each one in the sesame seeds to coat well. Place the coated balls on the prepared pan and bake for 30 minutes.

Sauce

2½ cups vegetable broth

¼ cup unsalted tomato paste

1 to 2 tablespoons tamari

2 cloves garlic, crushed

½ teaspoon garlic powder

½ teaspoon onion powder

½ teaspoon dried thyme

½ teaspoon dried marjoram

Pinch cayenne

½ cup cashews, finely ground

2 teaspoons freshly squeezed lemon juice

Salt

Freshly ground pepper

6. To make the sauce, combine the vegetable broth, tomato paste, tamari, garlic, garlic powder, onion powder, thyme, marjoram, and cayenne in a 2-quart saucepan. Bring to a boil over medium-high heat. Decrease the heat to medium and simmer 1 to 2 minutes.

7. Add the cashews, whisk and cook for 4 to 5 minutes, or until the sauce has thickened. The sauce will continue to thicken upon standing. Before serving, stir in the lemon juice, salt, and pepper.

8. To serve, spoon the sauce into a large, deep platter and arrange the tornadoes over the sauce. To garnish, poke a rosemary sprig into each tomato half and push them into the tops of the tornadoes so they stand upright.

Note: If not serving immediately, refrigerate the tornadoes and sauce separately. Warm the tornadoes in a preheated 350-degree F. oven for 12 to 15 minutes before serving. Heat the sauce in a saucepan over medium heat for 4 to 5 minutes.

Holy Moly Posole

Posole is a hearty main-dish soup served throughout Mexico on Christmas Eve to recognize life's blessings. When served on New Year's Day, posole is thought to bring good luck.

½ cup raw pumpkin seeds

1¼ pounds fresh tomatillos, husks removed

3 cups vegetable broth or water

1 (14-ounce) can diced tomatoes

2 large fresh tomatoes, chopped

1 large onion, chopped

3 large cloves garlic, coarsely chopped

½ to 2 jalapeño chiles, minced

2 teaspoons ground cumin

1 teaspoon ground coriander

1 teaspoon garlic powder

1 teaspoon dried oregano

½ teaspoon chili powder

1 large zucchini, chopped, or 4 ounces green beans, cut into 1-inch lengths

1 red bell pepper, or 1 carrot, chopped

1. Preheat the oven to 350 degrees F. Put the pumpkin seeds in a single layer on a 17½ x 12½-inch rimmed baking sheet. Bake for 8 minutes or until toasted. Alternatively, toast the pumpkin seeds in a skillet over high heat, stirring constantly for 1½ to 2 minutes. Immediately transfer them to a plate to cool. Put the seeds in a blender or food processor. Process until ground to a fine meal.

2. Wash the tomatillos under running water. (They will retain their somewhat sticky surface.) Slice them into quarters and put them in an 8- to 10-quart stockpot.

3. Add the vegetable broth, the canned and fresh tomatoes, onion, garlic, jalapeño, cumin, coriander, garlic powder, oregano, and chili powder. Cover and bring to a boil over high heat. Decrease the heat to medium, uncover, and simmer for 10 to 12 minutes.

4. Add the zucchini and bell pepper and cook 5 to 8 minutes. Add the black beans, pinto beans, hominy with liquid, salt, and the reserved ground pumpkin seeds and cook another 5 minutes to thicken the posole.

1 (15-ounce) can black beans, drained and rinsed

1 (15-ounce) can pinto beans, drained and rinsed

1 (1-pound, 13-ounce) can hominy, undrained, or 1 (15-ounce) can corn kernels, undrained

½ to 1 teaspoon salt

Lemon juice

1½ cups Tofu Sour Cream (page 83)

5. Before serving, add the lemon juice and adjust the seasonings. Ladle the posole into large soup bowls and place a dollop of Tofu Sour Cream into each serving. Serve the add-ins of your choice on the side.

Add-ins: Sliced radishes, chopped onions, shredded lettuce, shredded green cabbage, diced avocados, sliced green or black olives, crushed baked tortilla chips, steamed or roasted chopped chayote squash, hot sauce, shredded vegan jack, Cheddar, or nacho cheese, lime wedges, dried oregano, chopped cilantro

Savory Chickpea Yule Log

Mention yule log and most people picture a sweet, cream-filled cake roll frosted to look like a log of wood. Rebel that I am, I present a Christmas yule log that can be prepared in advance and served warm or chilled as a delicious, savory main dish, lunch dish, or even an appetizer.

1 large onion, minced

5 cloves garlic, minced

1½ teaspoons dried basil

1 teaspoon curry powder

1 teaspoon ground cumin

1 teaspoon salt

½ teaspoon ground pepper

¼ teaspoon dried thyme

3 tablespoons tamari

1 tablespoon extra-virgin olive oil

1 tablespoon freshly squeezed lemon juice

1¾ cups chickpea flour

1½ teaspoons dried basil

1½ cups tofu

⅓ cup sliced kalamata olives

Tofu Sour Cream (page 83) or 1 cup Asian Mustard Sauce (page 113)

Garnishes

1 large or 2 small Roma tomatoes, thinly sliced, slices halved

8 sliced kalamata olives

2 tablespoons minced fresh parsley

1. Line a 9 x 5 x 3-inch loaf pan with enough plastic wrap to drape generously over the sides.

2. Combine the onion, garlic, basil, curry powder, cumin, salt, pepper, and thyme in a large, deep skillet. Add the tamari, oil, and lemon juice and cook and stir over high heat for 3 to 4 minutes or until the onion is soft and transparent. Decrease the heat to medium-high.

3. Add the chickpea flour and about ½ cup of the water at a time, stirring constantly with a wooden spoon until the mixture is smooth. Decrease the heat to medium and cook for 18 to 20 minutes, stirring frequently, until the mixture reaches the consistency of very thick porridge and begins to pull away from the sides and bottom of the skillet.

4. Add the sliced olives and stir well to distribute them evenly. Spoon the chickpea mixture into the prepared loaf pan, pressing firmly with the back of the spoon to close any air pockets. Let cool for 1½ to 2 hours to create a firm pâté.

5. Invert the pâté onto an oval or rectangular dish and remove the plastic wrap. With your hands, mold it into the shape of a yule log.

6. To garnish, if desired, surround the log with some of the tomato slices and top each tomato slice with an olive slice. Top the yule log in the same manner. Sprinkle the outer edges of the dish with minced parsley if desired. Cut the yule log into ½-inch to ¾-inch slices and serve with Tofu Sour Cream or Asian Mustard Sauce on the side.

Wild Rice and Chestnut Pilaf

Makes 4 to 6 servings

Chestnuts are the definitive sweet infusion that makes this earthy pilaf so special, while exotic spices help transform it into a vibrant side dish.

3¼ cups water

1 cup wild rice

1¾ teaspoons salt

1 large red onion, coarsely chopped

2 tomatoes, chopped

¼ to ¾ teaspoon curry powder

½ teaspoon ground cinnamon

½ teaspoon garam masala

¾ cup chopped cooked and peeled chestnuts, or coarsely chopped raw or roasted walnuts

1 green onion, sliced, for garnish

1 tablespoon minced fresh parsley, for garnish

1. Combine 3 cups of the water, wild rice, and 1 teaspoon of the salt in a 4-quart saucepan. Cover and bring to a boil over high heat. Decrease the heat to medium and simmer for 45 to 55 minutes, or until the rice is tender and most of the water is absorbed.

2. Meanwhile, combine the onion, tomatoes, the remaining ¾ cup water, curry powder to taste, the remaining ¼ teaspoon salt, cinnamon, and garam masala in a large, deep skillet. Cook and stir over high heat for 5 to 8 minutes, or until the onion and tomatoes are softened. Add 1 or more tablespoons of water as needed to prevent burning.

3. Drain any excess liquid from the rice and add the rice and chestnuts to the tomato mixture. Mix well to distribute the ingredients evenly. Spoon the pilaf into a serving bowl and garnish with the green onion and parsley if desired.

Christmas Carrot Wreath

Makes 6 servings

You'll be tempted to sing "Deck the Halls" when this gorgeous golden wreath comes to the table.

12 ounces carrots (about 3 large), sliced

½ cup vanilla or plain soy milk

1½ teaspoons rice vinegar, cider vinegar, or white vinegar

⅓ cup canola oil

1 tablespoon plus 1 teaspoon freshly squeezed lemon juice

½ teaspoon almond extract

1¼ cups whole wheat pastry flour

⅓ cup light brown sugar, firmly packed

1 teaspoon baking powder

½ teaspoon baking soda

½ teaspoon salt

Garnishes

1 bunch parsley, cilantro, or mint

⅓ cup diced red bell pepper

2 tablespoons sliced almonds

1. Preheat the oven to 350 degrees F. Lightly oil a 4-cup metal ring mold.

2. Put the carrots in a 2-quart saucepan with enough water to cover them. Cover and bring to a boil, immediately decrease the heat to medium and simmer for 5 to 6 minutes, or until the carrots are fork-tender.

3. Meanwhile, combine the soy milk and vinegar in a medium bowl and set aside for 5 minutes to thicken slightly. Stir in the oil, lemon juice, and almond extract. Set aside.

4. Using a slotted spoon, drain carrots thoroughly and transfer them to a bowl. Mash them well with a fork or potato masher. Measure 1 cup of the mashed carrots and set aside. Use any remaining carrots for another recipe.

5. Combine the flour, brown sugar, baking powder, baking soda, and salt in a large bowl and mix well.

6. Add the mashed carrots and soy milk mixture to the dry ingredients and mix thoroughly. Spoon the carrot batter into the prepared mold and bake for 25 to 30 minutes, or until a toothpick inserted into the center comes out clean. Let cool for about 10 minutes. Invert onto a serving platter.

7. To garnish, form a wreath of parsley around the perimeter of the serving platter platter and sprinkle with the bell pepper and almonds if desired.

Brussels Sprouts Go Seoul Searching

Add a little Seoul to the holiday table with a platter of Brussels sprouts bathed in an exotic blend of Asian seasonings.

SEE PHOTO BETWEEN PAGES 26–27

2 pounds Brussels sprouts

3 tablespoons tamari or soy sauce

3 large cloves garlic, crushed

1 tablespoon plus 1 teaspoon maple syrup

1 tablespoon sesame oil

1 green onion, chopped

1 teaspoon toasted sesame seeds plus 1 teaspoon for garnish

Pinch cayenne

1. Fill a 4- to 6-quart saucepan two-thirds full with water. Cover and bring to a boil over high heat. Meanwhile, trim the Brussels sprouts stems and discard. Cut the sprouts in half lengthwise. Plunge the sprout halves into the boiling water in batches and boil for 1½ minutes. Use a slotted spoon to transfer them to a bowl and repeat the process until all the sprouts are tender. Drain any water from the bowl and set aside.

2. Combine the tamari, garlic, maple syrup, sesame oil, onion, 1 teaspoon of the sesame seeds, and cayenne in a large, deep skillet. A few minutes before serving, bring the sauce to a boil and add the Brussels sprouts. Cook and stir constantly for 1 to 2 minutes to coat the Brussels sprouts and heat them through.

3. Transfer the sprouts to a serving platter or bowl. Garnish with a sprinkle of the remaining 1 teaspoon of toasted sesame seeds if desired.

Glazed Beets in Maple-Balsamic Sauce

Makes 4 to 5 servings

Though beets are a year-round root vegetable, winter is when they're the most welcomed at the table. They taste great when bathed in balsamic vinegar and maple syrup.

SEE PHOTO BETWEEN PAGES 26–27

3 large beets (1½ to 2 pounds), peeled and cut into ½-inch cubes

1 large onion, coarsely chopped

½ cup water

Salt

Freshly ground pepper

2 tablespoons balsamic vinegar

2 tablespoons maple syrup

1 teaspoon freshly squeezed lemon juice

Strip lemon or orange peel, for garnish

1. Combine the beets, onion, and water in a large, deep skillet and cook and stir over high heat for 12 to 15 minutes. Add 1 or more tablespoons of water as needed to cook the beets until fork-tender; there should be no water remaining. Sprinkle lightly with salt and pepper.

2. Add the balsamic vinegar, maple syrup, and lemon juice to the skillet and cook and stir frequently for 2 to 3 minutes over high or medium-high heat until glazed. Transfer the beets to a serving bowl, and garnish with lemon peel if desired. Serve warm, chilled, or at room temperature.

Garlicky Roasted Cauliflower

Makes 6 servings

Many of us know people who shake their heads and wrinkle their noses at the mention of cauliflower. Slip them a taste of this dish and they turn into cauliflower devotees.

SEE PHOTO BETWEEN PAGES 26–27

2 heads cauliflower

1 green bell pepper, chopped

½ red bell pepper, diced

1 onion, cut in half vertically, then sliced into half-moons

½ cup pitted kalamata olives, halved lengthwise

12 cloves garlic, cut in half lengthwise

2 to 3 tablespoons extra-virgin olive oil

1 tablespoon freshly squeezed lemon juice

Salt

Freshly ground pepper

6 tablespoons Homemade Parmesan (page 114) or prepared vegan Parmesan

½ bunch parsley, for garnish

5 slices orange or tangerine, for garnish

1. Preheat the oven to 375 degrees F. Cut the cauliflower into bite-sized florets and put them in a large ziplock bag. Add the bell peppers, onion, olives, garlic, and oil. Seal the bag and shake well to coat the vegetables.

2. Arrange the vegetables in a single layer on a 17½ x 12½-inch rimmed baking sheet and roast them for 15 minutes. Turn the vegetables with a spatula and roast another 10 to 15 minutes, or until the cauliflower is fork-tender and lightly browned.

3. Toss the cauliflower mixture with the lemon juice and season with salt and pepper. Transfer to a serving platter and sprinkle with Homemade Parmesan. Garnish with parsley and orange slices if desired.

Old Saint Nick's Wicked Walnut Cookies

Makes 4½ dozen

With a generous measure of creamy puréed walnuts, these delicious cookies offer melt-in-the-mouth soft centers and delightfully crunchy outsides.

2 cups raw walnuts

3 cups whole wheat pastry flour

1¼ cups organic sugar

1 cup old-fashioned rolled oats

½ cup raisins

1 teaspoon baking powder

½ teaspoon baking soda

¼ teaspoon ground cinnamon

**1 cup mashed bananas
(about 2 large)**

⅔ cup vegan margarine

**1¼ teaspoons black walnut extract,
maple extract, almond extract, or
another 1 teaspoon vanilla extract**

1 teaspoon vanilla extract

¼ cup water

**2 tablespoons flaxseeds or
ground flaxseeds**

1. Preheat the oven to 350 degrees F. Line two 17½ x 12½-inch rimmed baking sheets with parchment paper.

2. Chop ½ cup of the walnuts into small pieces and set aside. Combine the flour, sugar, oats, raisins, baking powder, baking soda, and cinnamon in a large bowl and mix well. Make sure the raisins are well coated with flour to prevent them from sinking to the bottom of the batter. Set aside.

3. Put the remaining 1½ cups of walnuts in a food processor. Process until they become a creamy walnut butter, stopping occasionally to scrape down the work bowl. Add the bananas, vegan margarine, black walnut extract, and vanilla extract and process until smooth and creamy, stopping occasionally to scrape down the work bowl.

4. Add the wet ingredients to the dry ingredients and mix well. The dough will become quite stiff.

5. Pour the water and flaxseeds in a blender. Process on high speed for 1 to 2 minutes to form a thick slurry. Stir the slurry into the dough, mixing thoroughly to distribute it evenly.

6. Roll teaspoonfuls of dough into 1-inch balls and place them 1½ inches apart on the prepared baking sheet. Flatten them slightly with your hands or the bottom of a glass and press a piece of the reserved chopped walnuts into the center of each cookie.

7. Bake for 14 to 18 minutes or until the until the cookies are lightly browned on the bottom. If the cookies on the top rack need browning, move them to the bottom rack for another 2 to 3 minutes. Transfer the cookies to a cooling rack or plate and let cool completely.

Almond Thumbprint Cuties

Traditional thumbprint cookies are filled with fruity jam, but these little treats feature centers filled with dates and almond butter.

Cuties

1 cup almonds

1⅓ cups all-purpose flour

½ cup plus 2 tablespoons vegan margarine

½ cup plus 3 tablespoons organic sugar

2 tablespoons water

1 teaspoon almond extract

½ teaspoon vanilla extract

Filling

15 pitted dates, snipped in half

2 tablespoons almond butter

2 tablespoons water

½ teaspoon almond extract

½ teaspoon vanilla extract

1. Preheat the oven to 350 degrees F. Line two 17½ x 12½-inch rimmed baking sheets with parchment paper.

2. To make the cuties, put the almonds in a food processor. Process until they are ground into a finely textured meal. Add the flour, vegan margarine, sugar, water, almond extract, and vanilla extract, and process until well blended, stopping occasionally to scrape down the work bowl.

3. Roll heaping tablespoonfuls of dough into 1-inch balls and place them 1½ inches apart on the prepared baking sheet.

4. Use your thumb or finger to press a deep indentation into the top of each cookie. Use your fingers to smooth out any cracks in the dough. Bake for 12 to 15 minutes, or until the tops turn a light golden. Transfer the cookies to a cooling rack or plate and let cool completely.

5. To make the filling, put the dates, almond butter, water, almond extract, and vanilla extract in a food processor. Pulse to break up the dates, and then process until smooth and creamy, stopping occasionally to scrape down the work bowl.

6. Place heaping teaspoonfuls of the date mixture into each thumbprint. Set the cookies aside in a single layer for about 3 hours, or until the filling becomes firm and dry. Stored at room temperature in a covered container, Almond Thumbprint Cuties will keep for 1 or 2 days; refrigerated, for 1 week, and in the freezer, 3 months.

Pumpkin-Pine Nut Cookies

Makes 2½ dozen

These delightful pumpkin cookies give the tongue a little tingle and make ideal treats for holiday gifting.

1½ cups whole wheat pastry flour

1½ cups old-fashioned rolled oats

1 cup plus 2 tablespoons
dark brown sugar, firmly packed

2 teaspoons ground cinnamon

1½ teaspoons baking powder

1¼ teaspoons whole coriander
seeds, ground with a mortar
and pestle, or 1 teaspoon
ground coriander

1 teaspoon ground nutmeg

¾ teaspoon ground pepper

½ teaspoon baking soda

¼ teaspoon salt

¼ teaspoon cayenne

½ cup pine nuts

1¼ cups cooked fresh pumpkin
or canned pumpkin

½ cup canola oil

1 teaspoon vanilla extract

¼ cup water

2 tablespoons flaxseeds or
ground flaxseeds

1. Preheat the oven to 350 degrees F. Line two 17½ x 12½-inch rimmed baking sheets with parchment paper.

2. Combine the flour, oats, brown sugar, cinnamon, baking powder, coriander, nutmeg, pepper, baking soda, salt, and cayenne in a large bowl and mix well. Stir in the pine nuts and set aside.

3. Combine the pumpkin, oil, and vanilla extract in a medium bowl and mix well. Add the wet ingredients to the dry ingredients and mix well to form a thick dough.

4. Put the water and flaxseeds in a blender. Process on high speed for 1 to 2 minutes to form a thick slurry. Stir the slurry into the dough, mixing thoroughly to distribute it evenly.

5. Place heaping tablespoonfuls of dough 2 inches apart on the prepared baking sheets, spreading with the back of the spoon to form 1½-inch diameter cookies.

6. Bake for 15 minutes. Switch the top pan to the bottom rack and the bottom pan to the top rack, and bake another 13 minutes for soft cookies or about 17 minutes for crisp cookies. Transfer the cookies to a cooling rack or plate and let cool completely.

Pistachio Paradise Cookies

Makes 3 dozen

While on vacation in the Philippines, I began craving pistachios, but there wasn't a single one to be found. Instead, I found an array of tropical fruits and exotic spices that inspired these flavorful cookies.

2 cups whole wheat pastry flour

2 cups old-fashioned rolled oats

1 cup organic sugar

½ cup millet

1 teaspoon baking powder

1 teaspoon ground cardamom

1 teaspoon baking soda

¼ teaspoon saffron threads, crushed (optional)

¼ teaspoon salt

1½ cups pistachios

1 cup mashed bananas (about 2 large)

⅔ cup vegan margarine

2 to 3 tablespoons rose water or orange blossom water

1 tablespoon freshly squeezed lemon juice

1 teaspoon vanilla extract

¼ cup water

2 tablespoons flaxseeds or ground flaxseeds

1. Preheat the oven to 350 degrees F. Line two 17½ x 12½-inch rimmed baking sheets with parchment paper.

2. Combine the flour, oats, sugar, millet, baking powder, cardamom, baking soda, the optional saffron, and salt in a large bowl, mix well, and set aside.

3. Set aside ½ cup of the pistachios. Put the remaining 1 cup of pistachios in a food processor. Process until finely ground. Add the bananas, vegan margarine, rose water, lemon juice, and vanilla extract and process until the mixture is smooth and creamy, stopping occasionally to scrape down the work bowl.

4. Add the wet ingredients to the dry ingredients and mix well.

5. Pour the water and flaxseeds into a blender. Process on high speed for 1 to 2 minutes to form a thick slurry. Stir the slurry into the dough, mixing thoroughly to distribute it evenly. The dough will become quite stiff.

6. Place heaping tablespoonfuls of dough 2 inches apart on the prepared baking sheets. Flatten them slightly with your hands or the bottom of a glass and press one reserved pistachio into the center of each cookie.

7. Bake for 13 minutes. Switch oven rack positions of the pans and bake another 4 minutes or until the cookies are nicely browned on the bottom. If the cookies on the top rack need browning, move them to the bottom rack for another 2 to 3 minutes. Transfer the cookies to a cooling rack or plate and let cool completely. The cookies will firm when completely cooled.

8. Covered with plastic wrap, Pistachio Paradise Cookies will keep for 3 days at room temperature. Wrapped between layers of waxed paper and stored tightly covered in the freezer, they will keep for 3 months.

Santa's Favorite Panforte

Makes about 20 servings

Baked into slabs, dusted with powdered sugar, and cut into bite-sized chunks, these crunchy, chewy nut- and fruit-filled nuggets make joyful treats for everyone. You will need a candy thermometer for preparing the syrup.

Panforte

2 cups pecans

1¾ cups walnuts

1¼ cups almonds

1 cup dried apricots (preferably Turkish), diced

1 cup all-purpose or whole wheat pastry flour

¾ cup plus 2 tablespoons organic sugar

½ cup raisins

½ cup chopped dates

½ cup sweetened dried cranberries

2 tablespoons plus 1½ teaspoons ground cinnamon

1 cup powdered sugar

1. Preheat the oven to 350 degrees F. Line four 8-inch metal or aluminum foil pie pans, or 7-inch cake pans with parchment paper.

2. To make the panforte, spread the pecans, walnuts, and almonds on a 17½ x 12½-inch rimmed baking sheet and toast them for 8 minutes. Immediately transfer the nuts to a large platter to cool and decrease the oven temperature to 325 degrees F.

3. Combine the apricots, flour, sugar, raisins, dates, cranberries, and cinnamon in an extra-large bowl. Add the cooled nuts and toss well to coat all the ingredients. Set aside.

Syrup

1 cup agave nectar

¾ cup plus 2 tablespoons organic sugar

4. To make the syrup, combine the agave nectar and organic sugar in a 2-quart saucepan and mix well. Attach the candy thermometer to the side and place the pan over medium-high heat. Boil until the temperature reaches 230 degrees F, about 5 minutes. (This can happen very quickly.) Do not stir.

5. Immediately pour the syrup into the fruit-nut mixture and use a heavy-duty wooden spoon to stir and coat the ingredients well. The mixture quickly becomes extremely stiff, and you'll need to apply muscle power to combine the syrup and fruit-nut mixture thoroughly.

6. Distribute the mixture equally among the prepared pans, placing one spoonful of the mixture in the pan at a time, packing it down before adding another. Bake for 25 to 30 minutes. Let cool completely before removing from the pans. Carefully remove the parchment paper from each slab and dust each heavily with powdered sugar on both sides, using your hands to coat it completely.

7. To serve, use a sharp, heavy-duty knife to cut the panforte into 1-inch pieces or slice into thin wedges. Wrapped in a double layer of plastic wrap at room temperature, Santa's Favorite Panforte will keep for 3 months, or for 1 year in the refrigerator.

Chocolate Truffle Mousse
with Cranberry Splash

Makes 8 servings

You can serve this dessert as a simple mousse without the Cranberry Splash and top it with a fresh strawberry or a small cluster of thawed frozen raspberries and a sprig of fresh mint for garnish—but you'll be missing a special flavor burst from one of the great jewels of the fall and winter season. SEE PHOTO BETWEEN PAGES 26–27

Mousse

2 cups water

1 cup cashews

⅓ cup coconut cream or full-fat coconut milk

1 cup plus 1 tablespoon organic sugar

1½ teaspoons vanilla extract

½ teaspoon ground cinnamon

8 ounces unsweetened vegan chocolate

Splash

1½ cups fresh cranberries

1½ cups water

¾ cup plus 1½ tablespoons organic sugar

8 small sprigs fresh mint leaves, for garnish

1. To make the mousse, pour the water and cashews into a blender. Process for 1 to 2 minutes, or until smooth and creamy, stopping occasionally to scrape down the blender jar. Add the coconut cream, sugar, vanilla extract, and cinnamon and set aside in the blender.

2. Put the chocolate in a 1- or 2-quart saucepan. Cook and stir over the lowest heat for 1 to 2 minutes, or until the chocolate is completely melted. Add the melted chocolate to the blender. Process until the mousse is smooth and creamy, stopping occasionally to scrape down the blender jar. Spoon the mousse into eight small dessert cups or long-stemmed glasses to within ½ inch of the tops. Chill for 8 to 12 hours to firm. Wash and dry the blender jar.

3. To make the splash, combine the cranberries, water, and sugar in a 2-quart saucepan and bring to a boil uncovered over high heat. Decrease the heat to medium and simmer 12 to 15 minutes.

4. Let cool for 10 minutes. Transfer the cranberry mixture to a blender. Process until smooth, stopping occasionally to scrape down the blender jar. Pour the cranberry mixture into a small pitcher or serving bowl and chill for 8 to 12 hours. Because of its natural pectin, it will firm slightly when refrigerated.

5. To serve, stir the splash vigorously and spoon a generous portion over the chocolate truffle. Top with a mint sprig if desired.

Spiced Cranberry Nog

Makes about 3½ cups; 5 punch-cup servings

A sinfully delicious, festive holiday beverage, this unique take on eggnog unveils a tangy edge and an inviting hue of powder-puff pink, thanks to the cranberries.

1½ cups fresh cranberries

2 cups vanilla soy milk

¾ cup maple syrup

2 teaspoons ground cinnamon

1 teaspoon vanilla extract

½ teaspoon ground allspice

¼ teaspoon ground nutmeg

¼ teaspoon ground cloves

⅛ teaspoon xanthan gum or guar gum

1. Put all the ingredients in a blender. Process on high speed for 1 minute, or until the cranberries are completely broken down and the nog becomes thick and creamy, stopping occasionally to scrape down the blender jar. (Tiny flecks of cranberries may be visible.)

2. Pour the nog into a pitcher and refrigerate until ready to serve. Covered and refrigerated, Spiced Cranberry Nog will keep for 3 days.

Wassail

Makes 10 (1-cup) servings

This slowly mulled, ale-based punch is the perfect warming beverage to offer your guests when they've just come in from the cold.

10 cups apple cider

3½ to 4 cups dark beer or ale

¾ to 1 cup organic sugar

4 or 5 (3-inch) cinnamon sticks

1 (1-inch) piece fresh ginger, peeled and sliced

1 whole nutmeg

3 whole cardamom pods

2 or 3 lemon slices

1. Combine the apple cider, beer, sugar, cinnamon, ginger, nutmeg, and cardamom in an 8- to 10-quart stockpot and bring to a boil over high heat. Immediately decrease the heat to medium-low and simmer very gently for 20 to 30 minutes.

2. Add the lemon slices and keep the wassail warm on the lowest heat until ready to serve. Serve in punch cups or coffee mugs.

Hot Mulled Grape and Pomegranate Punch

Makes 8 servings

This joyful season can also be blustery and begs for a warm, lightly spiced, pleasantly sweet beverage to bring welcoming comfort when guests visit for the holiday celebration.

4 cups grape juice

4 cups pomegranate juice

½ cup light brown sugar, firmly packed

1 tablespoon plus 1 teaspoon pomegranate molasses

4 (3-inch) cinnamon sticks

16 whole allspice

2 dashes hot sauce

Pinch cayenne

2 or 3 lemon slices, for garnish

2 or 3 orange slices, for garnish

1. Combine the grape juice, pomegranate juice, brown sugar, pomegranate molasses, cinnamon sticks, allspice, hot sauce, and cayenne in a 6- to 8-quart stockpot and bring to a boil over high heat. Decrease the heat to medium and simmer gently for 5 minutes.

2. Ladle the punch through a fine-mesh strainer into a pitcher or small punch cups. If serving in a punch bowl, remove the cinnamon sticks and allspice and float the lemon and orange slices on the surface if desired.

CHAPTER 3

Hanukkah:
A Celebration of Lights, Latkes, and Dreidels

HANUKKAH, THE FESTIVAL OF LIGHTS, is a joyful holiday that commemorates a miraculous event that occurred in ancient Jerusalem in 165 BCE, when the Jews, led by a revered leader named Judah Maccabee, chased the Syrian army out of Jerusalem and regained possession of their temple.

They searched through the ruins for the holy olive oil to relight their eternal light that, to this day, hangs above the altar in every Jewish temple. Fortunately, they found a small bottle of consecrated oil, but there was only enough to last a single day. Miraculously, that single little bottle of oil burned for eight days. Judah Maccabee proclaimed a special eight-day festival to commemorate the miracle of the lights and called it Hanukkah, meaning "dedication."

The traditional Hanukkah celebration begins with the lighting of a nine-candle menorah. Eight of the candles represent the eight miraculous days the little vial of oil burned in the ancient temple. The ninth candle, the *shamash*, is used to light the other eight. On the first night, the shamash lights one candle. On the second night, the shamash lights two candles, and so on, until, on the eighth night, all the candles are burning.

To celebrate this holiday, many families exchange gifts all eight nights. Each year, families retell the story of Hanukkah, sing songs, and play the dreidel game with a special spinning top.

The unwritten yet traditional Hanukkah menu almost always includes foods fried in oil in remembrance of the miracle.

Sweet and Sour Cabbage Borscht

Makes 5½ quarts; 12 soup-course servings; 8 main-dish servings

While the base of this borscht features a thin beet broth, the many chunky vegetables, potatoes, and beans make the soup robust and wholesome. And, don't forget the Tofu Sour Cream.

1 pound beets (5 or 6 small), peeled and diced

12 cups water

2 teaspoons salt

1 bay leaf

1 clove garlic, crushed

2 to 3 large carrots, cut into ½-inch slices

2 cups cooked white beans, or 1 (15-ounce) can cannellini beans, drained and rinsed

1 (28-ounce) can tomatoes, coarsely chopped

2 stalks celery, cut into ½-inch slices

1 green bell pepper, chopped

1. Put the beets, water, salt, bay leaf, and garlic in a 10- to 12-quart stockpot. Cover and bring to a boil over high heat. Decrease the heat to medium-high and simmer 20 to 25 minutes, or until the beets are fork-tender.

2. Add the carrots, beans, tomatoes, celery, bell pepper, potato, onion, and cabbage to the stockpot. Cover and bring to a boil over high heat. Decrease the heat to medium and simmer about 20 minutes, or until the vegetables are tender.

1 large potato, scrubbed and cut into bite-sized chunks

1 onion, chopped

1 small head green cabbage (about 1½ pounds), cut into quarters and cut into ½-inch slices

⅓ to ½ cup dark brown sugar, firmly packed

⅓ to ⅔ cup freshly squeezed lemon juice

1½ cups Tofu Sour Cream (page 83)

3. Season with the brown sugar and lemon juice. Ladle the soup into bowls and place a dollop of Tofu Sour Cream into each serving.

Mushroom-Barley Cholent

Makes 6 to 8 servings

There are as many versions of cholent as there are inventive cooks. This vegan version of the traditional Jewish Sabbath stew dresses in humble schmates *(rags) but promises not to disappoint.*

2 large onions, sliced, slices cut into quarters

½ cup water

3 or 4 cloves garlic, crushed

1 (3-inch) cinnamon stick

⅔ cup pearl barley

1 pound shiitake mushrooms (10 to 12)

1 (1-pound, 2-ounce) package chicken-style seitan, or 12 ounces to 1 pound extra-firm tofu, cut into ¾-inch chunks

4 potatoes (preferably Yukon gold), scrubbed and cut into quarters

3 large carrots, sliced

6 to 8 cloves garlic, crushed

5 cups vegetable broth

1¼ teaspoons salt

¾ teaspoon paprika

½ teaspoon ground ginger

1. Preheat the oven to 400 degrees F.

2. Combine the onions, water, and crushed garlic in a large, deep skillet. Cook and stir over medium-high heat for 12 to 15 minutes, or until the onions are translucent and beginning to turn golden brown. Add 1 or more tablespoons of water as needed to prevent burning.

3. Transfer the cooked onions to a 6-quart, covered casserole, place the cinnamon stick in the onions, and sprinkle with the barley.

4. Remove and discard the mushroom stems. Cut the mushroom caps in half and add them to the casserole with the seitan, potatoes, carrots, and garlic.

5. Combine the vegetable broth, salt, paprika, and ginger in a medium bowl and pour the mixture over the vegetables. Cover and bake for 1 hour and 15 minutes.

Carrot and Sweet Potato Tzimmes

Makes 4 to 5 servings

The traditional definition of tzimmes *is "a big deal" or "a big fuss." A tzimmes is not a big deal but rather a simple peasant dish that almost always includes dried prunes or dried apricots.*

1 onion, cut into 8 wedges

1 pound carrots, peeled and coarsely shredded

1 (15-ounce) can chickpeas, drained, liquid reserved

1 red potato, scrubbed and cut into large chunks

8 ounces pitted prunes

1 pound sweet potatoes, peeled, cut into 1-inch chunks

¼ cup plus 2 tablespoons maple syrup

½ to ¾ teaspoon salt

½ teaspoon ground cinnamon

¼ teaspoon ground pepper

½ cup water

1½ teaspoons potato flour, cornstarch, or arrowroot starch

1 to 2 tablespoons coarsely ground walnuts, for garnish

1. Preheat oven to 375 degrees F.

2. Layer the vegetables in a 13 x 9-inch baking pan in the following order: onion, carrots, chickpeas, red potato, prunes, and sweet potatoes.

3. Add enough water to the chickpea liquid to equal 1½ cups. Add the maple syrup, salt, cinnamon, and pepper to the chickpea liquid, mix well, and pour it over the vegetables.

4. Cover the baking pan with aluminum foil and bake for 1 hour. Decrease the temperature to 325 degrees F and bake another hour.

5. Heat the water in a small saucepan over medium-high heat until simmering. Add the potato flour and whisk until it is well incorporated. Pour it evenly over the vegetables. Cover and bake another 20 to 30 minutes to thicken the liquid. Before serving, sprinkle with the walnuts if desired.

Old World Vegetable Goulash

When Eastern European Jews came to America during the early 1900s, they brought their food traditions with them and adapted their family recipes to ingredients available in their new homeland. I've borrowed from many regions of the Old and New Worlds to create this sumptuous stew, or goulash, the well-known Hungarian dish.

5¾ cups water

1 cup pearl barley

1½ teaspoons salt

1 cup untoasted or toasted buckwheat

3 stalks celery, cut into ½-inch slices

2 onions, thickly sliced, cut into halves

12 cloves garlic, cut in half lengthwise

4 cups vegetable broth

1½ pounds green cabbage, coarsely chopped (about 9 cups)

2 large carrots, cut into thick slices

2 rutabagas or turnips, peeled and cut into bite-sized pieces

12 ounces white potatoes, scrubbed and cut into bite-sized pieces

8 ounces extra-firm tofu or tempeh, cut into ½-inch cubes (optional)

1. Pour 3 cups of the water, barley, and ¾ teaspoon of the salt in a 2-quart saucepan. Cover and bring to a boil over high heat. Decrease the heat to low and simmer for 50 to 55 minutes or until the barley is tender. Set aside.

2. Pour 1¾ cups of the remaining water, buckwheat, and the remaining ¾ teaspoon salt in another 2-quart saucepan. Bring to a boil over high heat. Decrease the heat to low and simmer for 15 to 20 minutes. Set aside.

3. Combine the remaining 1 cup water, celery, onions, and garlic in an 8- to 10-quart stockpot. Cook and stir over medium-high heat for 12 to 15 minutes, or until the vegetables are softened and beginning to turn golden. Add 1 or more tablespoons of water as needed to prevent burning.

1 tablespoon paprika

1 teaspoon dried marjoram

1 teaspoon dried oregano

Freshly ground pepper

1 (14-ounce) can diced tomatoes

8 ounces fresh or frozen edamame, shelled

1 (6-ounce) can unsalted tomato paste

1 tablespoon tamari

1 to 2 tablespoons freshly squeezed lemon juice

1½ cups Tofu Sour Cream (page 83)

8 to 10 sprigs fresh dill weed, for garnish

4. Add the broth, cabbage, carrots, rutabagas, potatoes, optional tofu, paprika, marjoram, oregano, and pepper. Cover and bring to a boil over high heat. Decrease the heat to medium and simmer gently for about 15 minutes.

5. Add the tomatoes, edamame, tomato paste, and tamari and simmer for 7 to 10 minutes. Season with lemon juice and salt and cook another 1 or 2 minutes to develop the flavors.

6. To serve, spoon ⅓ to ½ cup each of the barley and buckwheat into each soup bowl. Fill the bowls with the goulash. Place a dollop of Tofu Sour Cream and a sprig of dill in the center of each bowl if desired.

Potato Latkes with Tofu Sour Cream and Applesauce

Makes 16 to 20 (3-inch) latkes

No traditional Hanukkah party would be complete without latkes. Shredded potatoes oxidize quickly and turn dark, so have the rest of the meal prepared before making the latkes. SEE PHOTO BETWEEN PAGES 90–91

1 large sweet onion, coarsely chopped

2½ to 3 pounds russet potatoes, scrubbed and coarsely shredded

¼ cup matzoh meal

1½ teaspoons salt

1 teaspoon onion powder

½ teaspoon ground pepper

½ teaspoon garlic powder

1 to 1½ cups canola oil

1½ cups Tofu Sour Cream (page 83)

Applesauce

1. Line two large platters with a double layer of paper towels and keep more paper towels handy to place between the layers of the cooked latkes.

2. Put the onion in a food processor. Pulse until the onion is minced, stopping occasionally to scrape down the work bowl. Transfer the onion to a large bowl.

3. Add the potatoes, matzoh meal, salt, onion powder, pepper, and garlic powder to the bowl and mix well to distribute evenly.

4. Heat about ¼ inch of oil in two large skillets over medium-high to high heat. If using an electric frying pan, adjust the thermostat to 375 degrees F. When the oil is hot, drop 3 or 4 tablespoons of the potato mixture into the skillets and flatten the mixture slightly with the back of the spoon to form ½-inch thick latkes. (If the latkes are too thick, the outsides will be crisp but the insides will not be thoroughly cooked.) Cook 1 to 2 minutes, or until the bottoms are golden brown. Turn with a spatula and cook the other side until golden brown. Transfer the cooked latkes to the prepared platters.

5. Add oil to the skillets as needed and repeat the process until all the latkes are fried, placing paper towels between each layer on the platters. Serve with Tofu Sour Cream and applesauce.

Tofu Sour Cream

Makes 1½ cups

Use extra-firm silken tofu to create the closest replica to real sour cream.

1 (12.3-ounce) box extra-firm silken tofu, drained

¼ cup freshly squeezed lemon juice

½ teaspoon rice vinegar

¼ teaspoon salt

Put all the ingredients in a food processor. Process until smooth and creamy, stopping occasionally to scrape down the work bowl. Use immediately or refrigerate for 8 to 12 hours to thicken. Stored in a tightly covered container and refrigerated, Tofu Sour Cream will keep 1 week.

Beet Latkes

Makes 12 (3-inch) latkes

These burgundy-hued little beet cakes, perfumed with a hint of cinnamon, are delicately sweet and add a hearty touch to a light meal or can be served as a stand-in for a main dish.

2 large beets, peeled

1 pound soft tofu, well mashed

½ cup whole wheat pastry flour

½ cup minced onion

3 tablespoons organic sugar

1 teaspoon baking powder

1 teaspoon salt

¼ teaspoon ground pepper

¼ teaspoon ground cinnamon

1½ cups Tofu Sour Cream (recipe above)

1. Preheat the oven to 350 degrees F. Line a 17½ x 12½-inch rimmed baking sheet with parchment paper. Lightly oil the parchment paper.

2. Coarsely chop the beets and transfer them to a food processor. Pulse until they are minced, stopping occasionally to scrape down the work bowl.

3. Transfer the beets to a large bowl and add the tofu, flour, onion, sugar, baking powder, salt, pepper, and cinnamon. Mix well and spoon the beet mixture onto the parchment paper, forming patties about 3-inches in diameter.

4. Bake for 30 minutes. Turn the latkes with a spatula and bake for another 30 minutes. Serve with Tofu Sour Cream on the side.

Raisin-Nut Cabbage Rolls with Sweet and Sour Sauce

Makes 8 to 10 servings

While the venerated stuffed cabbage, or holishkes, *of Jewish tradition retains its wholesome, hearty, sweet and sour roots, it enjoys a delicious makeover for Hanukkah.*

Filling

2 cups plus 1 tablespoon water

¾ cup short-grain brown rice

1¼ teaspoons salt

2 onions, chopped

1 red bell pepper, chopped

2 cloves garlic, minced

14 ounces vegan sausage, or 8 ounces diced seitan

⅔ cup Brazil nuts, coarsely chopped

½ cup dark raisins, soaked in hot water to cover

½ cup golden raisins, soaked in hot water to cover

Freshly ground pepper

1. To make the filling, combine 2 cups of the water, rice, and ¾ teaspoon of the salt in a 2-quart saucepan. Cover and bring to a boil over high heat. Decrease the heat to low and simmer for 35 to 45 minutes, or until the rice is tender.

2. Meanwhile, combine the onions, bell pepper, garlic, and the remaining 1 tablespoon of water in a large, deep skillet. Cook and stir over high heat for 3 to 4 minutes, until the onions are just tender. Add 1 or more tablespoons of water as needed to prevent burning. Remove from the heat.

3. Crumble the vegan sausage into the skillet and add the nuts. Drain all the raisins well and add them and the remaining ½ teaspoon of the salt. Mix well to break up the vegan sausage chunks and add pepper to taste. Add the cooked rice to the skillet and mix well to distribute the ingredients evenly. Set aside.

Sauce

1 (15-ounce) can unsalted tomato paste

1½ cups water

¼ cup plus 3 tablespoons organic sugar

¼ cup plus 2 tablespoons freshly squeezed lemon juice

1½ teaspoons salt

Cabbage

1 large head green cabbage (2½ to 3 pounds)

4 cups water

1 to 2 tablespoons minced fresh parsley, for garnish

1 tablespoon toasted sesame seeds, for garnish

4. To make the sauce, combine the tomato paste, water, sugar, lemon juice, and salt in a 3-quart saucepan and simmer over medium heat for about 5 minutes to develop the flavors. Spoon in just enough of the sauce to cover the bottoms of two 13 x 9-inch baking pans. Set the remaining sauce aside.

5. To prepare the cabbage for filling, remove and discard any outer, damaged leaves. Using a paring knife, remove and discard the entire center core of the cabbage. Place the whole cabbage, core side down, in an 8- to 10-quart stockpot. Add the water. Cover and bring to a boil over high heat, decrease the heat to low, and simmer for 15 to 18 minutes, or until soft and pliable. Transfer the cabbage to a plate and let stand until it is cool enough to handle.

6. Preheat the oven to 350 degrees F. To form the cabbage rolls, separate the cabbage leaves one at a time by carefully lifting each one up from the core end. Place one leaf on a plate with the core end facing you. Spoon the filling into the center of the leaf. (The size of the cabbage leaf will dictate the amount of filling to use.) Roll up the core end first, tuck in the sides, and roll the leaf over to enclose it completely. Carefully place the cabbage roll, seam-side down, into the baking pans and repeat the process with the remaining cabbage leaves and filling. If the inner cabbage leaves are not tender enough, return the cabbage to the stockpot and simmer for another 3 to 5 minutes.

7. Spoon the remaining sauce over the tops of the cabbage rolls. Cover with aluminum foil and bake for 25 to 30 minutes. Before serving, sprinkle the cabbage rolls with the parsley and toasted sesame seeds if desired.

Horseradish Coleslaw

With the lively splash of prepared horseradish—considered a Jewish sinus treatment—and a touch of caraway seeds, this humble cabbage salad takes on a quintessential Eastern European flavor. SEE PHOTO BETWEEN PAGES 90-91

Coleslaw

4 cups coarsely shredded green cabbage

2 cups coarsely shredded red cabbage

1 large carrot, coarsely shredded

½ green bell pepper, diced

½ red bell pepper, diced

½ cup minced sweet onion

1 teaspoon caraway seeds (optional)

Paprika, for garnish

2 sprigs fresh dill weed, for garnish

Dressing

1 (12.3-ounce) box soft or firm silken tofu

4 tablespoons freshly squeezed lemon juice

2 tablespoons plus 1 teaspoon prepared vegan white horseradish

1 teaspoon salt

1 teaspoon rice vinegar

1. To make the coleslaw, mix cabbages, carrot, bell peppers, onion, and optional caraway seeds in a large bowl; set aside.

2. To make the dressing, put the tofu, lemon juice, horseradish, salt, and vinegar in a food processor. Process until smooth and creamy, stopping occasionally to scrape down the work bowl.

3. Pour the dressing over the coleslaw and toss until thoroughly combined. Transfer to a serving bowl, sprinkle with paprika and garnish with the dill if desired.

Cranberry and Winter Fruit Relish

Makes 5 to 6 servings

In festive Jewish meals, there is always something sweet served with the main course. This cheery and colorful fresh-fruit medley combines seasonal fruits with tart and pungent flavors and adds lively sweetness to the meal.

2 Fuyu persimmons, diced

1 Bosc pear, diced

¾ cup fresh cranberries

8 pitted dates, diced

5 tablespoons organic sugar

½ to 1 jalapeño chile, seeded and minced

1 tablespoon plus 1 teaspoon cider vinegar

1 clove garlic, minced

2 to 3 sprigs fresh mint, for garnish

Combine the persimmons, pear, cranberries, dates, sugar, jalapeño, vinegar, and garlic in a medium bowl and toss well to distribute the flavors and colors. Transfer the relish to a serving bowl and garnish with the mint if desired. Cover and refrigerate if prepared in advance.

Hanukkah Gelt Stir-Fry

Makes 4 to 5 servings

Nonvegetarian guests are often impressed with the lively colors of meals that come to my table and frequently ask how it's possible to keep the vegetables looking so bright. The secret is the brief "water-sauté" technique, as demonstrated in this recipe.

SEE PHOTO BETWEEN PAGES 90–91

12 ounces broccoli florets

8 ounces green beans,
cut into 1-inch lengths

8 ounces Brussels sprouts,
cut into quarters

6 shiitake mushrooms, stems
discarded and caps sliced

1 carrot, julienned

2 to 3 tablespoons water

Salt

Freshly ground pepper

¼ cup Homemade Parmesan
(page 114) or prepared
vegan Parmesan

¼ bunch parsley, for garnish

1 tomato wedge, for garnish

1. Combine the broccoli, green beans, Brussels sprouts, mushrooms, carrot, and water in a large, deep skillet. Cook and stir over high heat for 2 to 4 minutes, or just until crisp-tender. Add 1 or more tablespoons of water as needed to cook the vegetables and prevent burning.

2. Season with salt and pepper and transfer the vegetables to a serving dish. Sprinkle with Homemade Parmesan. Place the parsley at the edge of the dish and nestle the tomato wedge in the parsley if desired.

Eggplant with Creamy Beet and Horseradish Sauce

Makes 4 to 5 servings

Because of its pungency, horseradish, or chrain *in Yiddish, is often the center of discussion when it's passed around the table. Horseradish and beets have a natural affinity for each other and provide a unique accompaniment to simple baked eggplant slices.*

1 eggplant (about ¾ pound), peeled

½ cup cashews

1 cup water

¾ teaspoon salt

1½ cups canned beets, undrained, or freshly cooked diced beets with about ½ cup cooking liquid

3 to 4 tablespoons prepared vegan white horseradish

5 to 8 small sprigs fresh dill weed, for garnish

1. Preheat the oven to 375 degrees F. Line a 17½ x 12½-inch rimmed baking sheet with parchment paper.

2. Cut eggplant crosswise into ½-inch slices, and place the slices on the prepared baking sheet. Bake for 20 to 25 minutes, or until the eggplant is fork-tender.

3. Meanwhile, put the cashews and ½ cup of the water in a blender. Process on slow speed for a few seconds, then increase to high speed for 1 minute, stopping occasionally to scrape down the blender jar. Add the remaining ½ cup water and process until smooth and creamy. If you have a high-speed blender, put the cashews and all the water in at once and process on high speed.

4. Transfer the cashew sauce to a 1-quart saucepan and add the salt. Use a slotted spoon to transfer the beets to the sauce. Stir in a small amount of the beet liquid if needed to thin the sauce.

5. Bring to a simmer over medium heat, stirring constantly, for about 2 minutes, or until the sauce thickens. Adjust the heat as needed to prevent burning the sauce. Add the horseradish, mix well, and adjust the seasoning.

6. To serve, transfer the eggplant slices to a serving dish and spoon 2 to 3 tablespoons of the sauce onto each slice. Garnish the eggplant with the fresh dill if desired.

Pear and Walnut Compote with Choco-Wafers Makes about 6 servings

Holiday meals, whether at home or at my grandmother's, always concluded with a small bowl of stewed dried fruits perfectly sweetened and laced with cinnamon. Homemade Choco-Wafers turn this delicious, unpretentious compote into an elegant, alluring dessert. SEE PHOTO ON OPPOSITE PAGE

Wafers

1 cup walnuts

1 cup pitted dates, snipped in half

¼ cup plus 1 tablespoon water

3 tablespoons golden raisins

3 tablespoons plus 1 teaspoon unsweetened cocoa powder

1. To make the wafers, preheat the oven to 350 degrees F. Line a 17½ x 12½-inch rimmed baking sheet with parchment paper.

2. Put all the wafer ingredients in a food processor. Process until all the ingredients are well incorporated, the nuts are broken down to a fine, but slightly textured meal, and the mixture reaches a very thick, finely mashed, firm consistency, stopping occasionally to scrape down the work bowl.

3. Spoon the wafer mixture onto the prepared baking sheet and use the back of the spoon to form it into a ¼-inch thick rectangle approximately 8 inches by 9 inches.

4. Bake for 15 to 20 minutes, or until the wafer is set and almost dry to the touch but still soft. Remove from the oven and let cool completely. It will firm as it cools. When cool, cut into 2- or 3-inch squares and set aside until ready to serve, or put the squares in a ziplock bag and refrigerate.

(continued on page 91)

▶

Compote

2 fresh Anjou or Bosc pears, cored, cut into quarters, and sliced

1 cup fresh cranberries

½ cup plus 1 tablespoon light brown sugar, firmly packed

⅓ cup dark raisins

¼ cup plus 2 tablespoons freshly squeezed lemon juice

½ teaspoon ground cinnamon

½ teaspoon vanilla extract

¼ cup water

1 tablespoon cornstarch

3 tablespoons coarsely ground toasted walnuts, almonds, or hazelnuts, for garnish

5. To make the compote, combine the pears, cranberries, brown sugar, dark raisins, lemon juice, cinamon, vanilla extract,, and water in a 3- or 4-quart saucepan. Cover and bring to a boil over high heat. Immediately decrease the heat to low and simmer 10 minutes, or until the pears are softened.

6. To thicken the juice in the pan, combine the cornstarch and 1 tablespoon water in a small bowl or cup and stir until smooth. Stir the paste into the simmering compote a little at a time, stirring constantly, for about 1 minute, or until thickened to desired consistency.

7. To serve, spoon the compote into small dessert dishes and garnish each with the walnuts if desired. Tuck two wafers into the center or sides of the compote.

◄

Cranberry Apple Strudel

Ah, strudel! Decadently rich and oh, so revered! This strudel combines Old World tradition with New World cranberries.

Filling

1½ cups fresh cranberries

1 cup organic sugar

1 cup walnuts, coarsely chopped

⅔ cup almond meal

¾ cup dark raisins

½ cup golden raisins

1¼ teaspoons ground cinnamon

½ teaspoon ground cardamom

2 tablespoons freshly squeezed lemon juice

2 pounds Granny Smith or other tart apples, peeled, cut into quarters, and thinly sliced

1. Line a 17½ x 12½-inch rimmed baking sheet with parchment paper. Brush the parchment paper generously with canola oil and set aside.

2. To make the filling, put the cranberries, sugar, walnuts, almond meal, all the raisins, cinnamon, and cardamom in a large bowl and mix well.

3. Pour the lemon juice into a medium bowl and add the apples. Stir well, coating them completely with the lemon juice to prevent them from turning brown. Drain the apples, add them to the cranberry mixture and mix thoroughly. Set aside.

4. Preheat the oven to 350 degrees F. Place a dish towel horizontally on your workspace. Unroll the phyllo dough and place it on the dish towel. Cover it with another dish towel to prevent the phyllo from drying out. (Each time you remove a phyllo sheet, cover the dough with the dish towel.) Pour the canola oil into a small bowl and place it nearby.

5. Remove one sheet of phyllo, and place it on the counter horizontally in front of you. Using a pastry brush, lightly brush the dough with the oil. Remove a second sheet of phyllo, lay it over the top of the first sheet, and brush with oil. Repeat the process with three more phyllo sheets, using a total of five sheets.

Dough

15 sheets phyllo dough

⅓ cup canola oil

2 tablespoons organic sugar

¼ teaspoon ground cinnamon

6. Stir the filling well and drain any excess liquid. Spoon one-third of the filling horizontally across the center of the phyllo stack, leaving about 1½ inches on either end.

7. Lift up all five sheets of the horizontal edge of the dough nearest you and fold it over the filling. Tuck in both sides. Then roll up the strudel like a plump burrito, and place it onto the prepared pan, seam side down. Brush the top with canola oil. Repeat the process two more times and place all three strudels on the prepared baking sheet.

8. Combine the sugar and cinnamon in a small bowl and sprinkle the mixture over the tops of the strudels. Using a sharp serrated knife, cut 1½-inch wide slices halfway through each strudel.

9. Bake the strudels for 30 to 35 minutes, or until the phyllo is golden. Remove the pan from the oven and let cool for about 10 minutes. Using a serrated knife, cut completely through the slices and use a spatula to transfer them to a serving platter or individual serving dishes. Top each serving with a spoonful of Cranberry-Pear Compote (page 9) and a dollop of Satin Whipped Cream (page 36).

CHAPTER 4

Reflections on a Vegan Kwanzaa

THE KWANZAA HOLIDAY PAYS HOMAGE TO AFRICAN HERITAGE, CULTURE, AND TRADITION. Reflecting on their history, African-Americans recall how their ancestors were torn from their homeland during the sixteenth through nineteenth centuries, packed into crude, crowded vessels and shipped to the United States, the Caribbean, and parts of Latin America to work as slaves on plantations. Divorced from their families, their homes, and their traditions, the Africans lost their cultural identity. The traumatic experience also deprived them of their feelings of community and pride.

Dr. Maulana Karenga, professor and chairman of the Department of Black Studies at California State University, Long Beach, noting how African-Americans still struggle to find acceptance within the American melting pot, recognized the need for a holiday that could bring them together to celebrate their heritage. In 1966, he created Kwanzaa, a celebration that encourages reflection, builds pride and joy, and creates a sense of community that honors African-American ancestry.

The celebration and its rituals are designed to fulfill the social and spiritual needs of African-Americans. While still a new tradition, Kwanzaa, which means "first fruits" in Swahili, is spreading to the diaspora of African peoples living in Latin America, the United States, and throughout the world.

While the Kwanzaa celebration, from December 26 to January 1, includes joyful gatherings and some gift-giving, the holiday was conceived to set aside this special time for families and friends to come together and reflect on community, culture, and family.

Curried Pumpkin-Peanut Soup

Makes about 12 cups; 6 servings

Pumpkin is one of many symbolic vegetables featured during the Kwanzaa holiday, though the variety grown in Africa may be more akin to hearty kabocha squash than our familiar thin-fleshed American pumpkin.

2½ to 3 pounds pie pumpkin, kabocha squash, or butternut squash

1 large onion, diced

1 large carrot, diced

2 stalks celery, including leaves, chopped

½ cup water

2½ cups vegetable broth

½ cup unsalted chunky peanut butter

3 to 4 tablespoons organic sugar

1 tablespoon plus 2 teaspoons freshly squeezed lemon juice

1¾ teaspoons curry powder

1 teaspoon salt

2½ cups sweetened or unsweetened soy milk

1 green onion, sliced, for garnish

1. Preheat the oven to 400 degrees F. Line a 17½ x 12½-inch rimmed baking sheet with parchment paper.

2. Place the pumpkin on the prepared pan and bake for 1 hour, or until the pumpkin is soft when gently pressed. Let cool slightly.

3. Meanwhile, combine the onion, carrot, celery, and water in an 8- to 10-quart stockpot. Cook and stir over high heat for 3 to 5 minutes, or until the vegetables are softened. Add 1 or more tablespoons of water as needed to cook the vegetables and prevent burning.

4. Decrease the heat to medium and add the vegetable broth, peanut butter, sugar, lemon juice, curry powder, and salt. Whisk vigorously to incorporate the peanut butter completely.

5. Cut the pumpkin in half and discard the seeds. Scoop out the flesh and put it in a food processor in batches along with some of the soy milk. Process until smooth and creamy, stopping occasionally to scrape down the work bowl. Transfer the pumpkin to the stockpot, add any remaining soy milk, and whisk it into the soup.

6. Warm gently over medium heat. If needed, thin the soup to desired consistency with additional water, soy milk, or vegetable broth and adjust the seasonings. Ladle the soup into bowls and sprinkle each serving with green onion if desired.

Groundnut Stew

Because peanuts mature in their pods while underground, they earned the name "groundnuts." While they originated in South America, they reached African shores through the early Spanish and Portuguese explorers and became a hearty staple.

4 tomatoes, each cut into 8 wedges, or 1 (28-ounce) can diced tomatoes

3 to 4 cups chopped green cabbage

2 sweet potatoes or yams, peeled and cut into ¾-inch chunks

2 large carrots, sliced

1 large onion, cut in half vertically, then sliced into half-moons

2 cloves garlic, minced

4 cups vegetable broth or water

1 (6-ounce) can unsalted tomato paste

⅓ cup raisins

1 teaspoon salt

¼ teaspoon ground pepper

Pinch cayenne (optional)

¾ cup unsalted peanut butter

3 to 5 cups cooked brown rice, buckwheat, or millet

2 tablespoons crushed roasted peanuts, for garnish

1. Combine the tomatoes, cabbage, sweet potatoes, carrots, onion, and garlic in a large, deep skillet or 8- to 10-quart stockpot.

2. Pour in 3 cups of the vegetable broth and bring to a boil over high heat. Cook and stir for about 2 minutes. Decrease the heat to medium-low and simmer 10 to 15 minutes, or until the carrots and sweet potatoes are fork-tender.

3. Add the remaining 1 cup of vegetable broth, the tomato paste, raisins, salt, pepper, and the optional cayenne and stir well. Cook for 1 minute and add the peanut butter. Whisk vigorously to incorporate the peanut butter completely. Serve over rice and garnish each serving with a sprinkle of peanuts if desired.

Mac 'n' Cheese

A cherished dish in the African-American community, this long-standing Southern favorite is an easy sell with kids and adults as well.

SEE PHOTO FACING PAGE 27

8 ounces whole-grain penne

1 large onion, coarsely chopped

¼ cup water

1½ cups unsweetened soy milk

¾ teaspoon salt

Dash hot sauce

Freshly ground pepper

2 tablespoons cornstarch

2 tablespoons water

1¼ cups shredded vegan Cheddar or nacho-flavored cheese

1 cup shredded vegan jack or mozzarella cheese

2 tablespoons Homemade Parmesan (page 114) or prepared vegan Parmesan

¼ cup fine breadcrumbs

1. Preheat the oven to 350 degrees F. Lightly oil a 3-quart casserole.

2. Cook the penne according to the package directions. Drain well and transfer to the prepared casserole.

3. Combine the onion and water in a deep, nonstick skillet. Cook and stir over medium-high heat for 12 to 15 minutes, or until the onion is browned. Add 1 or more tablespoons of water as needed to cook the onion and prevent burning. When all the liquid in the skillet has evaporated, add the onion to the penne and toss well.

4. To make the sauce, combine the soy milk, salt, hot sauce, and pepper in a 2-quart saucepan and bring to a boil over medium-high heat. Decrease the heat to a simmer.

5. To thicken the sauce, combine the cornstarch and water in a small bowl or cup until smooth. Stir the paste into the simmering soy milk a little at a time, stirring constantly, for about 1 minute, or until thickened to desired consistency.

6. Add the vegan cheeses and stir for about 3 minutes, or until the cheeses are completely melted. Adjust the seasoning.

7. Pour the sauce over the penne mixture and sprinkle with the breadcrumbs. Bake for 20 minutes, or until bubbling.

Jamaican Jerk Tofu

Reflecting the diaspora of people of African descent now living in the Caribbean, this mildly spiced tofu dish offers tasty diversity to the celebration menu. Though this dish is easy to make, you'll need to start preparing it at least two days in advance to allow time to press and marinate the tofu. SEE PHOTO FACING PAGE 27

2 pounds firm or extra-firm tofu

1 large onion, coarsely chopped

4 green onions, coarsely chopped

¼ cup plus 2 tablespoons freshly squeezed lime juice

¼ cup maple syrup

¼ cup tamari

6 cloves garlic

2 tablespoons extra-virgin olive oil

1 tablespoon red wine vinegar

1 jalapeño chile, seeded and coarsely chopped

1 (1-inch) piece peeled fresh ginger, coarsely chopped

1 teaspoon ground cinnamon

1 teaspoon dried thyme

½ teaspoon ground nutmeg

½ teaspoon ground pepper

½ teaspoon ground allspice

¼ teaspoon ground cloves

¼ teaspoon cayenne

Garnishes

1 small bunch cilantro

2 red chiles

2 green chiles

1 yellow chile

1. To press the excess water from the tofu, line a 17½ x 12½-inch rimmed baking sheet with a triple layer of dish towels. Cut the tofu into ⅜-inch slices and put them on the towels. Cover the tofu with another triple layer of towels. Place a cutting board on top of the towels and weigh it down with two or three books or other items. Set aside at room temperature for 24 hours.

2. To make the marinade, put the onion, green onions, lime juice, maple syrup, tamari, garlic, olive oil, vinegar, jalapeño, ginger, cinnamon, thyme, nutmeg, pepper, allspice, cloves, and cayenne in a food processor. Process until the mixture is well mixed but still somewhat chunky, stopping occasionally to scrape down the work bowl. (If prepared in advance, pour the marinade into a container. Cover and refrigerate until the tofu is ready.)

3. Pour some of the marinade into a 13 x 9-inch baking pan. Arrange the tofu slices in the marinade and pour the remaining marinade over the tofu. Cover and refrigerate for 24 hours.

4. Preheat the oven to 400 degrees F. Place the tofu slices on a 17½ x 12½-inch rimmed baking sheet, along with the marinade that clings to the tofu. Bake for 30 minutes. Pour the remaining marinade into a small serving bowl.

5. Transfer the tofu to a serving platter. Garnish with the cilantro and colorful chiles if desired. Serve the marinade on the side.

Jamaican Rice and Peas

Makes 4 to 6 servings

The recipe provides a good basic start to this favored island dish, which Caribbean cooks love to perk up with their favorite herbs and spices. Consider adding one or more of the following: ¼ teaspoon allspice, two or more cloves of garlic, two chopped green onions, ½ teaspoon brown sugar, or one fiery chile, such as scotch bonnet.

SEE PHOTO FACING PAGE 27

1 onion, diced

1 jalapeño chile, seeded and minced

1 clove garlic, minced

½ teaspoon dried thyme

1 (14.5-ounce) can kidney beans, drained and rinsed

1 cup brown basmati rice

1¼ cups water or vegetable broth

1 cup low-fat coconut milk

¾ teaspoon salt

¼ cup chopped fresh parsley, for garnish

1 red chile, for garnish

1. Combine the onion, jalapeño, garlic, and thyme in a 3-quart saucepan. Add 2 tablespoons of water and cook and stir over medium-high heat for 4 or 5 minutes, or until the onion is soft and transparent. Add 1 or more tablespoons of water as needed to cook the onion and prevent burning.

2. Add the beans, rice, water, coconut milk, and salt. Cover and bring to a boil over high heat. Decrease the heat to low and simmer for 35 to 45 minutes, or until the rice is tender and the liquid is absorbed.

3. Transfer the mixture to a serving bowl and sprinkle with the parsley if desired. For the finishing touch, poke the tip of the red chile into the center, leaving the stem pointing upward if desired.

African Pumpkin Stew

Because each region of the African continent offers its unique style of cooking pumpkin or squash stew, variations are seemingly limitless.

1 kabocha squash (2½ to 3 pounds)

4 onions, coarsely chopped

2 large carrots, cut into ½-inch chunks

4 pounds tomatoes, diced

3½ cups water

2 teaspoons ground coriander

2 teaspoons ground cumin

2 teaspoons chili powder

1½ teaspoons salt

1 teaspoon dried thyme

1 teaspoon ground cinnamon

⅛ teaspoon ground cloves

Freshly ground pepper

1 bunch Swiss chard, ribs discarded, finely chopped

1 cup roasted, unsalted peanuts, coarsely chopped

½ cup chopped fresh mint

1 to 2 jalapeño chiles, minced

Juice of 1 lemon

Cayenne, for garnish

1. Cut the squash in half with a sharp knife. (It is not necessary to remove the skin, because it becomes tender when cooked.) Discard the seeds. Cut the squash into 1-inch chunks and put them in a stockpot.

2. Put the onions and carrots in a food processor. Process until minced. Transfer them to the stockpot.

3. Add the tomatoes, water, coriander, cumin, chili powder, 1 teaspoon of the salt, thyme, cinnamon, cloves, and pepper to the stockpot. Bring to a boil over high heat. Decrease the heat to medium or medium-low, partially cover and simmer for about 20 minutes.

4. Add the chard, ½ cup of the peanuts, mint, and jalapeño and cook another 5 to 10 minutes. Add the remaining ½ teaspoon salt and pepper to taste.

5. Before serving, add the lemon juice and mix thoroughly. Ladle the stew into bowls and garnish each serving with the remaining ½ cup peanuts and cayenne if desired.

Southern Cornbread

Light and delicately sweet, this cornbread is one you'll be proud to serve your most honored guests.

SEE PHOTO FACING PAGE 27

1 cup unsweetened plain or vanilla soy milk

1 tablespoon rice vinegar or white vinegar

1 cup finely ground cornmeal

1 cup all-purpose flour or whole wheat pastry flour

¼ cup organic sugar

2 teaspoons baking powder

1 teaspoon baking soda

½ teaspoon salt

Egg replacer and water to equal 3 eggs

¼ cup plus 2 tablespoons water

½ cup melted vegan margarine

1. Preheat the oven to 400 degrees F. Lightly oil an 8 x 8-inch baking pan.

2. Combine the soy milk and vinegar in a medium bowl and set aside to sour.

3. Combine the cornmeal, flour, sugar, baking powder, baking soda, and salt in a large bowl and mix well.

4. Combine the egg replacer and water in a small cup or bowl and beat with a fork until foamy. Add the egg replacer mixture to the soured soy milk, and whisk in the melted vegan margarine.

5. Add the wet ingredients to the dry ingredients and mix until well incorporated. Spoon the batter into the prepared baking pan.

6. Bake for 20 to 25 minutes or until a toothpick inserted near the center comes out clean. Let cool 10 minutes and cut into squares.

Hoppin' John

In the southern United States, diners eat black-eyed peas with the hope of good fortune in the coming year. If a person eats one black-eyed pea every day of the year, will he or she have 365 days of good luck? Perhaps!

2 cups dried black-eyed peas, soaked overnight, drained and rinsed

6¼ cups water or vegetable broth

1 clove garlic, minced

½ to 1 teaspoon red pepper flakes or hot sauce

1¾ teaspoons salt

1 cup brown basmati rice

1 sweet onion, chopped

¼ cup plus 1 tablespoon imitation bacon bits

1 teaspoon liquid smoke

¼ cup minced fresh parsley, for garnish

1. Pour the peas into a 10- to 12-quart stockpot. Add 4 cups of the water, garlic, pepper flakes, and ¾ teaspoon of the salt and bring to a boil over high heat. Decrease the heat to medium and simmer for 30 to 40 minutes, or until the peas are tender. Add 1 or more tablespoons of water as needed to cook the peas thoroughly and still leave 1 cup of liquid in the pot.

2. Meanwhile, combine the remaining 2¼ cups of the water, the rice, and the remaining 1 teaspoon salt in a 2-quart saucepan. Cover and bring to a boil over high heat. Decrease the heat to low and simmer for 40 to 50 minutes, or until the rice is tender and all the water is absorbed.

3. Put the onion and 2 or 3 tablespoons of water in a large skillet. Cook and stir over medium-high heat for 12 to 15 minutes, or until the onion begins to turn golden. Add 1 or more tablespoons of water as needed to prevent burning. Set aside.

4. Add the cooked rice and onion to the peas. Stir in the imitation bacon bits and liquid smoke and mix well. Adjust the seasonings. Transfer to a serving bowl and garnish with the parsley if desired.

Mustard Greens with Tempeh Bacon

Makes about 4 servings

These humble greens symbolize money when eaten with black-eyed peas on the first day of the new year. The liquid remaining in the bottom of the pot is known in the South as "pot likker" and makes a tasty dipping sauce for bread.

1 (8-ounce) bunch mustard greens

1½ cups water

1 cup coarsely chopped onion

½ cup chopped green bell pepper

¾ teaspoon organic sugar

½ teaspoon salt

2 teaspoons canola oil

⅓ cup chopped tempeh bacon or imitation bacon bits

1. Remove and discard the tough stems of the mustard greens and coarsely chop the leaves. Put the greens in a 4-quart saucepan.

2. Add the water, onion, bell pepper, sugar, and salt and cover the saucepan. Bring to a boil over high heat. Decrease the heat to low and simmer for 30 minutes.

3. Meanwhile, heat the oil in a 10-inch skillet over high heat. Add the tempeh bacon and cook and stir frequently for 4 or 5 minutes, or until it is almost crisp.

4. Stir the tempeh bacon into the cooked greens. Using a slotted spoon, transfer the greens to a serving bowl. Pour the pot likker into another bowl so guests can dip their bread into it.

Okra Creole

Makes about 8 servings

Featuring tomatoes, onions, and a hint of peppery spice, this homey side dish makes a great pairing with Mac 'n' Cheese (page 98) along with a generous chunk of Southern Cornbread (page 102).   SEE PHOTO FACING PAGE 27

1 large onion, sliced

1 small green bell pepper, chopped

¼ cup water

1 clove garlic, minced

1 bay leaf

½ teaspoon dried thyme

¼ teaspoon red pepper flakes, or pinch cayenne

2 to 3 tomatoes, coarsely chopped

1 cup canned or frozen corn kernels, thawed

2 pounds cut or whole frozen okra, thawed

Salt

Freshly ground pepper

1 green onion, sliced, for garnish

1. Combine the onion, bell pepper, water, garlic, bay leaf, thyme, and pepper flakes in a large, deep skillet. Cook and stir over medium-high heat for about 5 minutes, or until the vegetables are just softened. Add 1 or more tablespoons of water as needed to cook the vegetables and prevent burning.

2. Add the tomatoes and corn. Decrease the heat to medium and cook another 7 to 10 minutes to soften the tomatoes and create a thick sauce.

3. Add the okra and cook about 3 minutes, or until just tender. Season with salt and pepper and transfer to a serving bowl. Sprinkle with sliced green onion if desired.

Sweet Potato Pie with Cashew-Ginger Cream

Makes 1 (9-inch) pie; 6 to 8 servings

From main dishes to side dishes to desserts, sweet potatoes bring charismatic soul to the Kwanzaa table. Contributing an exuberant new twist to the traditional dessert is the venturesome topping zapped with fresh ginger and creamy cashews.

SEE PHOTO FACING PAGE 27

Pie

1 Easy Pie Crust (page 107)

2 pounds sweet potatoes or yams, peeled and cut into bite-sized pieces

1 cup unsweetened soy milk

¼ cup arrowroot starch

¾ cup organic sugar

1½ teaspoons ground cinnamon

1½ teaspoons ground nutmeg

1 teaspoon vanilla extract

½ teaspoon ground ginger

Pinch salt

Cashew-Ginger Cream

1 cup cashews

¾ cup water

6 pitted dates, snipped in half

1 tablespoon organic sugar

2 teaspoons grated peeled fresh ginger

1 teaspoon vanilla extract

1. Preheat the oven to 350 degrees F. Prepare the Easy Pie Crust.

2. To make the pie filling, put the sweet potatoes in a 4-quart saucepan and add 1 cup of water. Cover and bring to a boil over high heat. Decrease the heat to low and cook for 5 to 7 minutes, or until the sweet potatoes are fork-tender. Alternatively, use a steamer to cook the sweet potatoes. Transfer the sweet potatoes to a large bowl and mash them well with a potato masher or fork.

3. Meanwhile, put the soy milk and arrowroot in a blender. Process briefly and set aside for 5 minutes to thicken.

4. Add the sugar, cinnamon, nutmeg, vanilla extract, ginger, and salt to the blender. Process until smooth and creamy. Pour the soy milk mixture into the mashed sweet potatoes and mix until thoroughly incorporated.

5. Spoon the sweet potato mixture into the prepared pie crust and smooth the top with the back of the spoon. Bake for 45 to 50 minutes, or until the filling is firm and the crust is golden. Let cool completely and refrigerate for 8 to 12 hours.

6. To make the Cashew-Ginger Cream, put the cashews, water, dates, sugar, ginger, and vanilla extract in a blender or food processor. Process until thick and creamy, stopping occasionally to scrape down the blender jar or work bowl. To serve, spoon over or next to a slice of pie.

Easy Pie Crust

1½ cups whole wheat pastry flour

½ cup ground flaxseeds

2 tablespoons organic sugar

½ teaspoon salt

½ cup canola oil

¼ cup plus 1 tablespoon water

1. Put the flour, flaxseeds, sugar, and salt in a food processor. Pulse several times to distribute the ingredients thoroughly. Add the oil and water and process until well mixed, stopping occasionally to scrape down the work bowl. Alternatively, combine the dry ingredients in a medium bowl, add the oil and water, and mix thoroughly by hand.

2. Spoon the crust mixture into a 9-inch pie pan. Use your fingers to press it into the bottom and up the sides of the pan.

CHAPTER 5

Happy New Year
Soup and Chili Bash

WHETHER MY NEW YEAR CELEBRATION BIDS FAREWELL TO THE "OLD" YEAR on New Year's Eve or welcomes in the "new" year on New Year's Day, I can bet the celebrants will be in a festive mood and ready for some tasty bites and zesty beverages.

Because many friends enjoy going out to dinner before the party, I plan to start the New Year's Eve gatherings on the late side, making for a perfect evening of nibbling on finger foods. And, of course, I provide plenty of party beverages for toasting. For the earlier crowd, a more substantial meal might include informal, make-ahead foods with a couple of salad dishes to round out the meal. Something sweet and a hot beverage guarantee a warm and happy conclusion to the festivities.

I am always mindful of the football fans who won't want to miss that exciting moment when their team scores a touchdown. Simple foods, such as bread and soup or chili, allow them to enjoy the festivities while glued to the TV, so two or three weeks in advance, I make a few breads, freeze them, and defrost them the night before the gathering. Then I make sure there are two giant stockpots of deliciously robust soups simmering on the stove at my open house.

I recognize today's busy lifestyles leave many of us little time to spend preparing complicated dishes, so I always welcome easy preps and am grateful when guests offer to bring "a little something." I consider it a blessing and accept it graciously.

And when the last guest says goodbye, I reflect on the old year, bid my personal farewell, and then look ahead with hope for a great new year.

Tasty Two-Finger Tidbits

Sometimes you just gotta turn your back on the fancy stuff and get down and dirty with the simplest, easiest, earthiest little appetizers that involve absolutely no cooking. Haul out the toothpicks, grab your paring knife, and create a host of tasty, pungent morsels that are just plain fun to eat.

Caper-Stuffed Dates

Makes 12 servings

12 pitted dates

12 caperberries with stems

Cut a lengthwise slit in each date. Press a caperberry into the opening of each date. Arrange them on a platter.

Tofu Skewers *SEE PHOTO FACING PAGE 91*

Makes 12 servings

**1 Fuyu persimmon,
cut into three slices**

**1 (7-ounce) package baked
teriyaki-flavored tofu**

**3 Spanish olives, cut into
quarters lengthwise**

Toothpicks

Cut the persimmon slices into quarters to make twelve portions. Cut the tofu into twelve ½-inch cubes. Form toothpick skewers with one piece of persimmon, one tofu cube, and one olive quarter. Arrange them on a platter.

Skewered Artichokes *SEE PHOTO FACING PAGE 91*

Makes 12 servings

3 canned, water-packed artichokes

**1 (10-ounce) package vegan nacho
cheese, cut into ½-inch cubes**

**1 crisp apple, cut into twelve
½-inch chunks**

Toothpicks

Cut artichokes lengthwise into quarters. Form toothpick skewers with one piece of artichoke, one piece of vegan cheese, and one piece of apple. Arrange them on a platter.

Apple and Bacon Morsels

Makes 12 servings

1 large crisp apple

1 (7-ounce) package tempeh bacon, cut into twelve 1-inch strips

12 walnut halves

Cut the apple crosswise into six slices; cut the slices in half, discarding seeds. Place a piece of tempeh bacon on each apple slice and place a walnut half on top. Arrange them on a platter.

Red-Robed kalamatas *SEE PHOTO FACING PAGE 91*

Makes 12 servings

12 pitted kalamata olives

4 pitted dates, each cut lengthwise into thirds

1 large roasted red bell pepper, sliced into 12 strips

Toothpicks

Hold an olive and a date piece together. Wrap a strip of roasted pepper around them and secure with a toothpick. Arrange them on a platter.

Sweet Potato Puffs

Makes 24 puffs; 10 to 12 servings

You'll be tempted to call these mini muffins the cutest little appetizers you've ever seen, and you'll be absolutely right. These savory pixie puffs have two attributes—eye appeal and irresistible flavor. SEE PHOTO BETWEEN PAGES 90–91

12 ounces sweet potatoes or yams, peeled and cut into bite-sized chunks

½ cup vanilla soy milk

1½ teaspoons rice vinegar or white vinegar

1¼ cups almonds

1 cup old-fashioned rolled oats

1¼ teaspoons salt

1 teaspoon baking powder

½ teaspoon baking soda

½ teaspoon ground cinnamon

½ teaspoon ground pepper

½ teaspoon garlic powder

¼ teaspoon ground cardamom (optional)

½ cup well-mashed firm tofu (about 5 ounces)

1. Preheat the oven to 350 degrees F. Place two mini muffin pans on a 17½ x 12½-inch rimmed baking sheet and set aside.

2. Bring the sweet potatoes to a boil in a covered 2-quart saucepan with enough water to cover the potatoes.. Decrease the heat to medium and simmer for 5 to 7 minutes, or until the sweet potatoes are fork-tender.

3. Meanwhile, combine the soy milk and vinegar in a small bowl and set aside to sour.

4. Put the almonds in a food processor. Process until coarsely ground. Transfer them to a large bowl and add the oats, salt, baking powder, baking soda, cinnamon, pepper, garlic powder, and optional cardamom. Mix well.

5. Drain the sweet potatoes and put them in the food processor with the tofu. Process until smooth and creamy, stopping occasionally to scrape down the work bowl. Transfer the sweet potato mixture to a medium bowl, add the soured soy milk and oil, and mix well.

6. Put the water and flaxseeds in a blender. Process on high speed for 1 to 2 minutes to form a thick slurry. Add the slurry to the sweet potato mixture and mix well. Add the sweet potato mixture to the dry ingredients and mix thoroughly to form a soft dough.

2 tablespoons canola oil

¼ cup water

1 tablespoon ground flaxseeds

1 green onion, minced

1 or 2 Roma tomatoes,
sliced and cut into quarters

7. Fill each muffin cup to heaping, pressing firmly with the back of a spoon to close any air pockets.

8. Sprinkle the green onion over the muffins, pressing them in lightly. Poke the point of a tomato quarter into the center of each puff so it stands up.

9. Bake for 40 to 45 minutes, or until firm. Let the puffs cool for 25 to 30 minutes in the pan. Serve with Asian Mustard Sauce for dipping.

Asian Mustard Sauce
Makes 1 cup

¼ cup water

¼ cup rice vinegar
or white vinegar

¼ cup maple syrup

2 tablespoons dry mustard

1½ teaspoons salt

¼ teaspoon xanthan gum
or guar gum

Put all the ingredients in a blender. Process for 1 minute. Transfer the sauce to a small serving bowl for dipping. Tightly covered and refrigerated, Asian Mustard Sauce will keep for 1 month.

Asian Pea-Pistachio Butter

If you're a shoot-from-the-hip, last-minute cook, you'll be glad you have this zesty starter in your recipe file. Just remember to thaw the peas, and you'll have this appetizer on the table in five minutes flat. Just add crackers.

1½ cups frozen peas, thawed

½ cup pistachios

2 tablespoons toasted sesame seeds

2 teaspoons tamari

2 teaspoons freshly squeezed
lemon juice

½ teaspoon five-spice powder

Pinch cayenne

1 whole radish, radish slices,
or radish rose, for garnish

1. Put the peas, pistachios, sesame seeds, tamari, lemon juice, five-spice powder, and cayenne in a food processor. Process for 1 to 2 minutes, or until the mixture is thick, well blended, and lightly textured, stopping occasionally to scrape down the work bowl.

2. Spoon the spread into a serving bowl, garnish with the radish if desired, and serve with your favorite crackers on the side.

Homemade Parmesan

Often I've come to rely on a sprinkle of vegan Parmesan to add sparkle to a dish, soup, a casserole, or an appetizer. With only five ingredients, this recipe is almost instant to make and tastes enough like the real thing to put the Italian touch on everything from pizza to minestrone and a host of holiday or everyday dishes.

1 cup almonds

1 tablespoon plus 1½ teaspoons
nutritional yeast flakes

1 teaspoon onion powder

1 teaspoon salt

½ teaspoon garlic powder

1. Put the almonds in a food processor. Process until they are finely ground yet still retain a bit of texture, stopping occasionally to scrape down the work bowl. (Avoid overprocessing or it will turn into almond butter.)

2. Add the nutritional yeast, onion powder, salt, and garlic powder and pulse until well mixed. Transfer to a covered container and refrigerate until ready to use. Covered and refrigerated, Homemade Parmesan will keep for 3 months.

Tempeh Bacon-Stuffed Mushrooms

Makes 4 to 5 servings

These flavorful mushrooms with their heaping hickory-seasoned stuffing do a great job of setting the scene for the delectable meal ahead. Assemble them a day in advance and serve them chilled or warm. SEE PHOTO BETWEEN PAGES 90-91

**8 large button mushrooms
(2 to 2½ inches in diameter)**

2 cups water

2 tablespoons tamari

⅓ cup coarsely chopped cashews

6 strips tempeh bacon

⅔ cup finely diced tomatoes

4 green onions, minced

**1 slice whole wheat bread,
cut into ⅛-inch cubes**

**1 tablespoon freshly squeezed
lemon juice**

¼ teaspoon liquid smoke

Pinch cayenne

Salt

Freshly ground pepper

Lettuce leaves

**8 thin strips yellow or orange
bell pepper, for garnish**

1. Remove the stems from the mushrooms. Save them for another use. Line a plate with a double layer of paper towels and set aside.

2. Pour the water and tamari in a large, deep skillet and bring to a boil over high heat. Add the mushroom caps and boil 3 to 5 minutes, turning the mushrooms halfway through. Drain the mushrooms on several layers of paper towels and set aside.

3. To make the stuffing, put the cashews in a food processor. Process until they are ground into a fine powdery meal. Transfer the cashew meal to a medium bowl.

4. Add the tempeh bacon, tomatoes, onions, bread, lemon juice, liquid smoke, cayenne, and salt and pepper to taste, and combine until the mixture is moist and the ingredients are distributed evenly.

5. Spoon a generous portion of the stuffing into each mushroom cap. Line a serving dish with lettuce leaves and arrange the stuffed mushrooms on the lettuce. Garnish each mushroom with a strip of yellow or orange bell pepper if desired.

New Year Logs in Spicy Pecan Gremolata

Makes 15 to 20 servings

Wearing a fragrant winter coat of pecans, coarse black pepper, and fresh herbs and served with crackers, this tasty log of well-seasoned tofu will delight a hungry crowd of party guests with a single schmear.

Gremolata

1 cup pecans

2 tablespoons coarse black pepper

2 tablespoons minced fresh parsley

2 tablespoons minced fresh dill weed

2 tablespoons finely chopped fresh chives

2 cloves garlic, minced

1 teaspoon minced lemon zest

¼ teaspoon salt

1. Preheat the oven to 350 degrees F.

2. To make the gremolata, spread the pecans in a single layer on a 17½ x 12½-inch rimmed baking sheet and toast them for 8 minutes. Immediately transfer them to a plate to cool. Put them in a hand-cranked nut mill and grind them into a coarse meal. Alternatively, pour the toasted pecans into a heavy-duty zip-lock bag, place the bag on a cutting board, and use a hammer to pound them into a coarse meal. Transfer the pecans to a medium bowl.

3. Add the pepper, parsley, dill, chives, garlic, zest, and salt to the pecans and mix well. Pour the gremolata mixture onto a large plate and set aside.

Logs

1 pound extra-firm tofu, drained

3 tablespoons unsweetened
soy milk or water

3 to 4 tablespoons freshly squeezed
lemon juice

1 tablespoon plus 1¼ teaspoons
rice vinegar

2 large cloves garlic, coarsely chopped

2 teaspoons onion powder

1¾ teaspoons salt

1½ teaspoons dried dill weed

1 teaspoon garlic powder

¾ teaspoon ground coriander

¼ teaspoon ground pepper

⅛ teaspoon cayenne

Sprigs of fresh dill weed, for garnish

3 small radishes or cherry tomatoes,
for garnish

4. To make the logs, pat the tofu completely dry with paper towels. Put the tofu in a colander with a dish underneath. Put a small dish on top of the tofu and weigh it down with a heavy object for 1 to 2 hours to remove excess water.

5. Break the tofu into pieces and put them in a food processor with the soy milk, lemon juice, vinegar, garlic, onion powder, salt, dill, garlic powder, coriander, pepper, and cayenne. Process until the mixture is smooth and creamy but still quite firm, stopping occasionally to scrape down the work bowl.

6. Transfer the tofu mixture to a plate and use your hands to form two logs. If the mixture is too soft to work with, refrigerate it for 1 or 2 hours until it is firm enough to handle.

7. Carefully roll the logs in the gremolata, coating them all around, except for the ends.

8. To serve, place the logs on separate platters. Pile crackers on one side of each log and garnish the other sides with fresh dill and radishes if desired. Wrapped individually in plastic wrap and refrigerated, New Year Logs in Spicy Pecan Gremolata will keep for 3 to 4 days.

New Year's Resolution Soup

Makes 5 to 6 quarts; 10 to 12 servings

Whether you like your soup spicy or mild, packed with chunky bits or a simple broth, filled with lots of noodles or none of those slippery bean threads, don't hesitate to make adjustments. Choose the spice level, the seasonings, the quantity of veggies, and the noodles you like best.

4 ounces dry mung bean noodles (bean threads) or rice penne

4 ounces rice vermicelli

4 quarts water

14 leaves napa cabbage, chopped

2 carrots, diced

1 large onion, chopped

1 (5-inch) daikon radish, peeled and chopped

8 ounces shiitake mushrooms, stems discarded and caps sliced

12 ounces broccoli florets, chopped

1 (2-inch) piece fresh ginger, peeled and grated

3 cloves garlic, minced

½ to 1 teaspoon curry powder

1. Place the mung bean noodles and the vermicelli in separate large bowls. Cover them with at least 3 inches of hot water and set aside to soak while preparing the soup.

2. Pour the water into an 8- to 10-quart stockpot. Add the cabbage, carrots, onion, daikon, mushrooms, broccoli, ginger, garlic, curry powder, turmeric, and cayenne. Cover and bring to a boil over high heat. Decrease the heat to medium-high or medium and simmer gently for about 10 minutes.

3. Add the tamari and vinegar and cook another 5 to 10 minutes, or until the vegetables are just softened.

½ teaspoon ground turmeric

Pinch cayenne

¼ cup tamari

¼ cup seasoned rice vinegar

1 pound firm tofu, cut into
bite-sized cubes

2 green onions, sliced, for garnish

½ cup hulled sesame seeds,
for garnish

4. Drain the noodles, add them to the stockpot, and cook another 5 minutes, or until the noodles are fully softened. Add the tofu, cook 1 to 2 minutes to heat through, and adjust the seasonings. Garnish each serving with a sprinkle of green onions and sesame seeds if desired.

White Bean and Root Vegetable Soup
Makes 4 to 5 quarts; 6 to 8 servings

This delectable soup exudes homemade goodness with every bite. It's even better the next day when the flavors of cinnamon and star anise have had an opportunity to mingle leisurely.

1 cup dried Great Northern, flageolet, or peruano beans

2 onions, chopped

3 cloves garlic, chopped

7 to 8 cups water

3 large carrots, thinly sliced

1 large parsnip, thinly sliced

8 ounces green beans, cut into 1-inch pieces

1 (3-inch) cinnamon stick

3 whole star anise, or 2 whole cloves

½ teaspoon dried oregano

½ teaspoon dried marjoram

2 to 3 tablespoons nutritional yeast flakes

Salt

Freshly ground pepper

3 tablespoons cornstarch

3 tablespoons water

2 tablespoons finely chopped fresh parsley, for garnish

1 Granny Smith apple, diced, for garnish

1. Soak the beans in enough water to cover for 8 to 12 hours. Drain the beans and transfer to an 8- to 10-quart stockpot. Add half the chopped onions, the garlic, and 4 to 5 cups of the water. Bring the beans to a boil over high heat, uncovered. Immediately decrease the heat to medium and simmer for 50 to 60 minutes, or until the beans are tender. Add more water as needed to prevent the beans from boiling dry.

2. Meanwhile, combine the remaining 3 cups water, carrots, remaining onions, parsnip, green beans, cinnamon, star anise, oregano, and marjoram in a large, deep skillet and bring to a boil over high heat. Decrease the heat to medium-high and cook and stir about 8 to 10 minutes, or until the vegetables are tender.

3. When the beans are tender, add the cooked vegetables and any water remaining in the skillet to the stockpot. Add the nutritional yeast and season with salt and pepper. Heat the soup until gently simmering. Remove the star anise.

4. To thicken the soup, combine the cornstarch and water in a small bowl or cup and stir until smooth. Stir the paste into the simmering soup a little at a time, stirring constantly, for about 1 minute, or until thickened to desired consistency.

5. Ladle the soup into bowls and garnish each serving with a sprinkle of parsley and a teaspoonful of diced apples in the center if desired.

Sweet Potato Soup

Makes 4 to 5 quarts; 8 to 10 servings

This delicately sweet, thick, creamy, and seductive sweet potato soup always makes a roomful of hungry partygoers happy. Add some hearty breads or whole-grain crackers and serve with Garlicky Chestnut Butter (page 9) or Asian Pea-Pistachio Butter (page 114).

7 cups water

2½ pounds sweet potatoes or yams, peeled and cut into 1-inch chunks

1 large onion, coarsely chopped

½ teaspoon salt

⅛ teaspoon ground cinnamon

⅛ teaspoon ground nutmeg

Freshly ground pepper

¼ cup raisins, for garnish

¼ cup chopped toasted pecans, for garnish

1. Combine 4 cups of the water, sweet potatoes, and onion in an 8 to 10-quart stockpot. Cover and bring to a boil over high heat. Decrease the heat to medium and simmer for 10 to 12 minutes, or until the sweet potatoes are fork-tender.

2. Let cool briefly. Use an immersion blender to process the soup in the stockpot until smooth and creamy. Alternatively, put the soup in a food processor. Process in batches until smooth and creamy, stopping occasionally to scrape down the work bowl.

3. Return the soup to the stockpot. Stir in the salt, cinnamon, nutmeg, and pepper, and enough of the remaining 3 cups of water to reach desired consistency. Adjust the seasonings.

4. Warm the soup over medium-high heat, ladle into bowls and garnish each serving with raisins and pecans if desired.

Mulligatawny Vegetable Soup

Makes 12 to 14 cups; 6 to 8 servings

Mulligatawny soup originated with a meat- or chicken-based broth in East India. As the soup traveled to the West, different ingredients were added, reflecting the influences of many creative cooks. Tofu, an optional ingredient, makes the soup hearty enough to be the main dish.

1 large onion, chopped

1 large crown broccoli, chopped

2 large carrots, sliced

1 large green apple, cored and chopped

¾ cup water

1 stalk celery, sliced

½ cup chopped red or green bell pepper

1 tablespoon ground coriander

2 teaspoons ground cumin

1 teaspoon ground turmeric

4 cloves garlic, crushed

¼ teaspoon red pepper flakes

2 whole cloves

1. Put the onion, broccoli, carrots, apple, water, celery, bell pepper, coriander, cumin, turmeric, garlic, pepper flakes, and cloves in an 8- to 10-quart stockpot.

2. Cook and stir the vegetables over medium-high heat for 8 to 10 minutes, or until they are softened. Add 1 or more tablespoons of water as needed to prevent burning.

4 quarts vegetable broth or water

2 potatoes, scrubbed and diced

¼ cup freshly squeezed lemon juice

3 to 4 tablespoons tamari

2 cups low-fat coconut milk

8 ounces extra-firm tofu,
diced (optional)

Salt

Freshly ground pepper

2 tablespoons chopped fresh parsley,
for garnish

3. Add the broth, potatoes, lemon juice, and tamari and simmer about 10 to 12 minutes, or until the potatoes are softened.

4. Add the coconut milk and optional tofu, and cook another 1 or 2 minutes. Remove the cloves and season with salt and pepper. Ladle the soup into bowls and garnish each serving with a sprinkle of fresh parsley if desired.

Barn-Burner Chili

Hot, hearty, and often a bit flamboyant with spices, chili is the smart choice for a relaxed meal. If you don't have a slow cooker, assemble the chili in a 10- to 12-quart stockpot and simmer gently on the stovetop for about an hour to develop the flavors. *SEE PHOTO BETWEEN PAGES 90–91*

Chili

2 onions, chopped

2 green bell peppers, chopped

1 red bell pepper, chopped

1 large crown broccoli, coarsely chopped

1 large carrot, chopped

5 cloves garlic, coarsely chopped

2¾ cups water

1 tablespoon balsamic vinegar

1 tablespoon tamari

3 cups bite-sized chunks scrubbed white or red potatoes

3½ cups cooked dried kidney beans, or 2 (15-ounce) cans kidney beans, undrained

1½ cups cooked dried pinto beans, or 1 (15-ounce) can pinto beans, drained

1½ cups cooked dried black beans, drained, or 1 (15-ounce) can black beans, drained

2 (6-ounce) cans unsalted tomato paste

1. Combine the onions, bell peppers, broccoli, carrot, garlic, and ½ cup of the water in a large, deep skillet. Cook and stir the vegetables over medium-high heat for 5 to 7 minutes, or until the vegetables are softened and all the water has evaporated. Add 1 or more tablespoons of water as needed to prevent burning.

2. Add the balsamic vinegar and tamari, stir well, and transfer the vegetables to a slow cooker.

3. Put the potatoes and enough water to cover in a 2-quart saucepan. Cover and bring to a boil over high heat. Decrease the heat to medium-high or medium and simmer for 5 to 7 minutes, or until the potatoes are just fork-tender.

1 large tomato, chopped

2 to 4 tablespoons maple syrup

2 tablespoons chili powder

1 tablespoon plus 1 teaspoon ground cumin

1 tablespoon red wine vinegar

2½ teaspoons liquid smoke

1½ teaspoons salt

1 to 2 teaspoons freshly squeezed lemon juice

¼ to ½ teaspoon cayenne

¼ teaspoon ground pepper

2 dashes hot sauce (optional)

Toppings

1 (15-ounce) can corn kernels, drained

1 sweet onion, chopped

1 (8-ounce) can black olives, drained and chopped

2 cups shredded vegan Cheddar cheese

4. Using a slotted spoon, transfer the potatoes to the slow cooker and add the remaining 2¼ cups water, all of the beans, tomato paste, tomato, maple syrup, chili powder, cumin, vinegar, liquid smoke, salt, lemon juice, cayenne, pepper, and optional hot sauce. Mix well to distribute the ingredients evenly. Cover and cook on low for 6 to 8 hours.

5. Adjust the seasonings, and spoon the chili into serving bowls. Serve the toppings in separate bowls on the table or near the slow cooker and make the meal a self-serve chili-and-toppings bar.

Sicilian Chili, Two Ways

Makes 8 to 10 generous servings

There are two ways to cook this boldly flavored chili—in the slow cooker or on top of the stove.

2 onions, chopped

1 red bell pepper, chopped

1 yellow bell pepper, chopped

1 green bell pepper, chopped

5 cloves garlic, minced

2¼ cups water

2 large tomatoes, chopped

1 (28-ounce) can diced tomatoes

1 (8-ounce) can tomato sauce

1 (6-ounce) can unsalted tomato paste

1 teaspoon dried basil

1 teaspoon dried oregano

2 (15-ounce) cans chickpeas,
drained and rinsed

1 (15-ounce) can kidney beans,
drained and rinsed

Slow-Cooker Sicilian Chili

1. Cook and stir the onions, bell peppers, garlic, and ½ cup of the water in a large, deep skillet over high heat for 7 to 9 minutes, or until the vegetables are softened and the onions are transparent. Add 1 or more tablespoons of water as needed to prevent burning.

2. Transfer the cooked vegetables to a slow cooker. Add the fresh and canned tomatoes, tomato sauce, tomato paste, basil, oregano, chickpeas, zucchini, olives, salt, cayenne, pepper, and the remaining 1¾ cups water.

3. Mix well and cook on low for 6 to 8 hours. Adjust the seasonings, and serve with Homemade Parmesan and shredded vegan mozzarella on the side.

1 large zucchini, chopped

1 (6-ounce) can pitted black olives, cut in half

⅔ to 1 cup pitted green olives, cut in half

1½ teaspoons salt

Pinch cayenne

Freshly ground pepper

Homemade Parmesan (page 114) or prepared vegan Parmesan

1 (10-ounce) package shredded vegan mozzarella

Stockpot Sicilian Chili

1. Cook and stir the onions, bell peppers, garlic, and ½ cup of the water in an 8- to 10-quart stockpot over high heat for 7 to 9 minutes, or until the vegetables are softened and the onions are transparent. Add 1 or more tablespoons of water as needed to prevent burning.

2. Add the fresh and canned tomatoes, tomato sauce, tomato paste, basil, oregano, and the remaining 1¾ cups water and bring the mixture to a boil, stirring frequently. Decrease the heat to medium and simmer about 10 to 15 minutes to cook the tomatoes and develop the flavors.

3. Add the chickpeas, zucchini, and olives and simmer another 10 minutes, or until the zucchini is fork-tender. Season with salt, cayenne, and pepper. Serve with Homemade Parmesan and shredded vegan mozzarella on the side.

Old-Fashioned Chili

For parties, I make two pots of mild chili for the timid folks and two pots of the spicier variety for the stout-hearted souls. The spice level in this recipe is fairly mild. For a zestier bite, use 1 teaspoon of red pepper flakes and add an extra tablespoon of chili powder.

1 onion, chopped

1 large green bell pepper, chopped

1 large red bell pepper, chopped

2 to 3 tablespoons water

1 cup textured soy protein (TSP)

¾ cup boiling water

1 (28-ounce) can whole tomatoes, chopped

1 (15-ounce) can kidney beans, undrained

1 (15-ounce) can pinto beans, undrained

1 (15-ounce) can black beans, drained and rinsed

1 (1-pound) can chili beans, undrained

1 (6-ounce) can unsalted tomato paste

1½ teaspoons salt

3 tablespoons plus 1 teaspoon chili powder

1. Cook and stir the onion, bell peppers, and water in a large, deep skillet for about 5 minutes, or until the onions and peppers are softened. Add 1 or more tablespoons of water as needed to prevent burning. Transfer to a 10- or 12-quart stockpot.

2. Combine the TSP and the boiling water in a medium bowl and set aside for 5 to 10 minutes, or until the TSP has softened and absorbed the water.

3. Add the TSP, tomatoes, beans, tomato paste, salt, chili powder, cumin, coriander, tamari, maple syrup, and red pepper flakes to the stockpot. Bring to a boil over high heat. Decrease the heat to medium and simmer 30 to 40 minutes.

1 tablespoon plus 2 teaspoons ground cumin

2½ teaspoons ground coriander

2 tablespoons tamari

1 to 2 teaspoons maple syrup

¼ to ½ teaspoon red pepper flakes

Toppings

1 onion, chopped

1 bunch cilantro, finely chopped

1 (1-pound) can corn kernels, drained

1 (8-ounce) can black olives, chopped

4. Ladle the chili into bowls. Serve the toppings in separate bowls on the table or near the slow cooker and make the meal a self-serve chili-and-toppings bar.

Variation: To cook the chili in a slow cooker, follow Steps 1 and 2. Transfer all of the ingredients to a slow cooker, and cook on low for 6 to 8 hours.

Hot Spiced Cranberry Punch

Makes about 16 (1-cup) servings

Nothing says welcome quite like a cup or mug of comforting, hot and spicy mulled punch.

SEE PHOTO BETWEEN PAGES 90–91

8 cups sweetened or unsweetened cranberry juice

6 cups water

2 cups white grape juice concentrate

Organic sugar

4 (3-inch) cinnamon sticks

10 whole cloves

1 lemon, sliced, for garnish

Combine the cranberry juice, water, grape juice concentrate, sugar to taste, cinnamon sticks, and cloves in an 8- to 10-quart stockpot. Bring to a boil over high heat. Decrease the heat to medium and simmer for about 10 minutes. To serve, float the lemon slices on the surface if desired.

Brandied Holiday Nog

Makes 6 (6-ounce) servings

I often serve a tiny pitcher of extra brandy with this so guests can crank up the holiday spirit a notch or two. You can also serve this tasty nog without the brandy and still enjoy a well-spiced festive beverage.

2 cups vanilla soy milk

1 cup cashews

½ cup apple juice

¾ cup maple syrup

¼ cup brandy

1 teaspoon vanilla extract

1 teaspoon ground cinnamon

½ teaspoon ground nutmeg, plus more for garnish

½ teaspoon ground allspice

¼ teaspoon plus ⅛ teaspoon ground cloves

1. Put 1 cup of the soy milk and the cashews in a blender. Process on high speed for 1 minute, or until smooth and creamy.

2. Add the remaining 1 cup of soy milk, the apple juice, maple syrup, brandy, vanilla extract, cinnamon, nutmeg, allspice, and cloves and process until thick and creamy, stopping occasionally to scrape down the blender jar.

3. To serve, pour the nog into glasses and sprinkle each with a pinch of nutmeg if desired. If preparing in advance, pour the nog into a 1½-quart pitcher and refrigerate.

Note: The nog will thicken slightly and tends to separate when refrigerated. Refresh with a brief whirl in the blender or whisk vigorously just before serving.

Happy New Year Glögg

Makes about 25 (6-ounce) servings

Glögg is a traditional hot wine punch that originated in Scandinavia. The warming punch is still part Nordic holiday festivities. Start the glögg preparations early in the day to allow sufficient time for steeping.

8 cups water

3 to 4 (3-inch) cinnamon sticks

1 whole nutmeg

15 whole cloves

10 cardamom pods, peeled, seeds crushed in a mortar and pestle

1 (2-inch) piece fresh ginger, peeled

Zest of 1 orange

1 (750-ml) bottle ruby port wine

1 (750-ml) bottle Burgundy wine

Juice of 1 orange

½ cup organic sugar

½ cup brandy

1 pound raisins, for garnish

1 pound blanched almonds, for garnish

1. Pour the water into a 10-quart stockpot. Place a 5- or 6-inch square, double-layer piece of cheesecloth on the countertop and put the cinnamon sticks, nutmeg, cloves, cardamom seeds, ginger, and orange zest in the middle. Gather up the corners and edges, forming a pouch, and tie the gathered edges securely with string. Put the spice pouch in the stockpot.

2. Cover and bring to a boil over high heat. Decrease the heat to medium and simmer for 15 to 20 minutes. Set aside for 2 to 4 hours to steep.

3. Remove the spice pouch and discard. Add the wines, orange juice, and sugar and bring to a boil. Immediately decrease the heat to barely simmering to keep the glögg warm and retain the alcohol. Add the brandy and simmer until heated through, 3 to 5 minutes.

4. Ladle the glögg into small punch cups. Add 1 tablespoon of raisins and a few blanched almonds to each cup, if desired, and serve with spoons so guests can easily enjoy the traditional treats at the bottom of the cups. Alternatively, add the raisins and almonds to the simmering glögg and ladle them into the cups with the punch as you serve.

Note: The residue at the bottom of the bottle of port may end up in the punch. If you prefer a clear beverage, strain the punch through several layers of cheesecloth before serving. Once you've added the wine and brandy, it's important not to overheat the punch or the alcohol will evaporate.

Hazelnut-Cranberry Bread Pudding with Crème Anglaise

Makes 10 to 12 servings

With plenty of servings for a large gathering, this colorful, homespun dessert delivers pleasing bursts of juicy, divinely sweet and tart flavors with each delicious spoonful. SEE PHOTO BETWEEN PAGES 90–91

Bread Pudding

¾ cup whole blanched hazelnuts or slivered almonds

8 slices whole wheat bread

1 pound fresh cranberries

3 large Bosc or Anjou pears, cored, and sliced

1¼ cups plus 2 tablespoons brown sugar, firmly packed

1¼ cups plus 2 tablespoons water

2 (3-inch) cinnamon sticks

¾ cup golden raisins

½ cup vanilla or plain soy milk

¼ cup freshly squeezed lemon juice

1 teaspoon ground cinnamon

¾ teaspoon ground nutmeg

1. Preheat the oven to 350 degrees F. Lightly oil a 13 x 9-inch baking pan.

2. Pour the hazelnuts into a heavy-duty ziplock bag, place the bag on a cutting board, and use a hammer to gently break them into coarse pieces. Set aside. If using slivered almonds, measure them and set aside.

3. Break the bread into 1-inch pieces and put them in a very large bowl. Add the cranberries and pears.

4. Combine the brown sugar, water, and cinnamon sticks in a 2-quart saucepan. Bring to a boil over high heat. Decrease the heat to medium-high and simmer for 5 minutes to create a syrup. Let cool and add it to the bread mixture.

5. Add the raisins, soy milk, lemon juice, ground cinnamon, and nutmeg and mix well.

6. Spoon the bread mixture into the prepared baking pan and cover with aluminum foil. Bake for 45 minutes. Remove the foil, and stir the mixture to break up the cranberries. Sprinkle with the chopped hazelnuts, cover with the foil, and bake for another 15 to 20 minutes.

Crème Anglaise

2 cups unsweetened soy milk

¼ cup plus 2 tablespoons organic sugar

¾ teaspoon vanilla extract

Pinch salt

3 tablespoons cornstarch

3 tablespoons water

7. To make the Crème Anglaise, combine the soy milk, sugar, vanilla extract, and salt in a 2-quart saucepan. Bring to a boil over medium-high heat and decrease the heat to medium.

8. Combine the cornstarch and water in a small bowl or cup and stir until smooth. Stir the paste into the simmering soy milk mixture a little at a time, stirring constantly for 1 minute, or until slightly thickened. Remove from the heat and let cool. If not using immediately, cover and refrigerate for 8 to 12 hours to firm. Tightly covered and refrigerated, Crème Anglaise will keep for 5 days. Makes about 2¼ cups.

9. To serve, spoon the bread pudding into dessert dishes and ladle some Crème Anglaise over each serving.

Apricot, Date, and Hazelnut Sticky Pie

Makes 1 (9-inch) pie; 8 servings

When you blend dried fruits with hazelnuts, you've combined the seductive elements of an exceptionally sweet treat. But mingle the merry makings of four different fruits with the crunchy, roasted, chunky nuts, spice them up, bind them with a magical medley of sweeteners, and voilà!—a stunning pie for the holiday!

1 Easy Pie Crust (page 107)

1½ cups blanched hazelnuts

¾ cup toasted pecans

1 cup brown rice syrup

¼ cup organic sugar

¼ cup maple syrup

⅓ cup tapioca flour

1 cup golden raisins

¾ cup diced dates

⅔ cup diced dried apricots (preferably Turkish)

½ cup sweetened dried cranberries

1¼ teaspoons ground cinnamon

½ teaspoon minced orange or lemon zest

⅛ teaspoon salt

1 tablespoon freshly squeezed lime juice

½ teaspoon maple extract

1. Preheat the oven to 350 degrees F. Prepare the Easy Pie Crust.

2. To make the filling, pour the hazelnuts into a heavy-duty zip-lock bag, place the bag on a cutting board, and use a hammer to gently break them into coarse pieces. Transfer the hazelnuts to a large bowl. Break the pecans into pieces and add them to the hazelnuts.

3. Combine the brown rice syrup, organic sugar, and maple syrup in a 2-quart saucepan. Add the tapioca flour and stir well with a wooden spoon until the flour is completely incorporated. Set aside for 5 minutes to allow the tapioca flour to absorb some of the moisture.

4. Bring the syrup mixture to a boil over medium heat and boil for 5 minutes. Remove from the heat and set aside.

5. Add the raisins, dates, apricots, cranberries, cinnamon, orange zest, and salt to the nuts and toss well to distribute the ingredients evenly.

6. Stir the lime juice and maple extract into the syrup mixture and mix well. Pour the syrup into the fruits and mix thoroughly to coat all the ingredients. (The mixture will become very thick and sticky, and combining it completely will likely take the place of your daily workout.)

7. Spoon the filling into the prepared crust and bake for 35 to 40 minutes. Let cool for 4 to 6 hours to set completely. Use a sharp, heavy-duty knife to cut into wedges. To store, cover the pie with plastic wrap and refrigerate. Bring the pie to room temperature before serving.

Cinnamon-Peanut Butter Torte

Makes 10 to 12 servings

This torte is deliriously rich in flavor, densely packed with peanut butter, and perfectly accented with cinnamon to bring out its sweetness. The bonus for the host is that this tantalizing treat can be prepared several days in advance and left in the freezer until shortly before serving.

Crust

1½ cups whole almonds

1½ cups sweetened dried cranberries

4 to 5 tablespoons water

Filling

1⅓ cups pitted dates, snipped in half

1 cup smooth or chunky unsalted peanut butter

¾ cup well-mashed firm tofu

½ cup plain soy milk

¼ cup organic sugar

2 teaspoons ground cinnamon

½ teaspoon vanilla extract

2 tablespoons sweetened dried cranberries

1 tablespoon coarsely ground dry-roasted unsalted peanuts

6 to 8 sprigs fresh mint, for garnish

1. Cover the base of a 9-inch springform pan with a piece of parchment paper 2 inches larger. Snap the collar back onto the base, and cut away the excess paper with scissors. Lightly oil the sides of the pan and set aside.

2. To make the crust, put the almonds in a food processor. Process until they become a coarse, slightly chunky meal.

3. Add the cranberries and water and process until the cranberries are broken down into tiny bits and the mixture holds together when gently pressed, stopping occasionally to scrape down the work bowl. Add water 1 tablespoon at a time if the mixture is too dry to hold together. Spoon the crust mixture into the bottom of the springform pan and press the mixture firmly with the back of a spoon to distribute it evenly. Wash and dry the work bowl.

4. To make the filling, put the dates, peanut butter, tofu, soy milk, sugar, cinnamon, and vanilla extract in the food processor. Process until the mixture is smooth and creamy, stopping occasionally to scrape down the work bowl.

5. Using a rubber spatula, transfer the filling to the springform pan, spreading evenly over the crust.

6. Sprinkle the dried cranberries and peanuts on top and gently press them into the surface. Freeze the torte until firm, about 8 to 12 hours. Remove it from the freezer 10 to 15 minutes before serving.

7. Run a knife around the edge of the pan to loosen the torte. Place the pan on a large serving platter. Carefully remove the collar. Decorate the platter with the mint if desired and cut the torte into wedges.

Chewy Ginger Cookies

Makes 3 to 4 dozen

Nut-brown, sweet, ginger-infused cookies are such a traditional part of the holiday scene and always add a tantalizing spicy aroma to any gift package.

2 cups whole wheat pastry flour

1 cup organic sugar

1 tablespoon ground ginger

2 teaspoons baking soda

1¼ teaspoons ground cinnamon

¼ teaspoon ground allspice

¼ teaspoon ground cloves

¼ cup plus 2 tablespoons water

2 tablespoons ground flaxseeds or whole flaxseeds

½ cup vegan margarine

¼ cup molasses

1. Preheat the oven to 350 degrees F. Line two 17½ x 12½-inch rimmed baking sheets with parchment paper.

2. Combine the flour, sugar, ginger, baking soda, cinnamon, allspice, and cloves in a medium bowl and mix well.

3. Pour ¼ cup of the water and the flaxseeds into a blender. Process on high speed for 1 to 2 minutes to form a thick slurry. Transfer the slurry to a food processor and add the vegan margarine, molasses and the remaining 2 tablespoons of water. Process until smooth and creamy, stopping occasionally to scrape down the work bowl.

4. Add the flour mixture to the food processor. Pulse and process to mix well and form a thick dough.

5. With a spoon, drop heaping teaspoonfuls of dough 2 inches apart on the prepared baking sheets. Flatten them slightly with your hands or the bottom of a glass.

6. Bake for 12 minutes. Let cookies cool on the baking sheets 3 to 4 minutes, or until firm. Transfer the cookies to cooling racks or plates and let cool completely.

Glossary

Almond meal: Almond meal is merely finely ground almonds, used mostly as a flavorful addition to baked goods as well as nut, whole grain, and bean patties. Almond meal can easily be made at home by pulverizing almonds in a food processor. It will keep six months in a covered container in the refrigerator.

Arrowroot starch: Arrowroot starch is a fine, white powder made from a starchy, tropical root, used as a thickener. It is sometimes substituted for wheat flour in gluten-free baking or used in place of cornstarch for thickening gravies and sauces. Store it in a covered container at room temperature.

Brown rice syrup: Brown rice syrup is a sweetener with an ultra-thick consistency that defies its delicate flavor. It's perfect for sticky, gooey desserts because it also contributes to a firm texture when baked.

Caperberries: Caperberries are large capers—some the size of grapes—imported from Spain and found in jars in the gourmet food section or condiment aisle of supermarkets.

Chickpea flour: Chickpea flour is made when dried chickpeas—also called garbanzo beans—are ground into flour. Used in gluten-free cooking and as a thickener or binding agent, chickpea flour is also known as garbanzo bean flour, gram flour, besan, harina de garbanzo, and channa flour.

Chipotle chili powder: Ground, dried, smoked jalapeño chiles lend a smoky flavor with a touch of heat. A little chipotle chile powder goes a long way, unless you're a fearless fire-eater.

Edamame: Edamame are green Japanese soybeans sold fresh or frozen, cooked or uncooked, in the pod or shelled. High in fiber and protein, they make a tasty and gorgeous addition to salads and hot or cold dishes.

Egg replacer: Egg replacer is a vegan, gluten-free binding and leavening powder that is mixed with water and used as a substitute for eggs in baked goods.

Five-spice powder: Five-spice powder is an exotic blend of five or more spices that usually includes star anise, cinnamon, fennel, cloves, and black pepper. Use it sparingly—it's quite pungent. Add a pinch to soups, sauces, salads, stir-fries, bean dishes, and grains to bring depth to the flavors.

Guar gum and xanthan gum: Dried white powders, used interchangeably as thickeners and emulsifiers, guar and xanthan gums are particularly handy when making homemade salad dressings in a blender. Guar gum comes from the seeds of the cluster bean or guar plant grown in India; xanthan gum is made from fermented corn sugar.

Hominy: Hominy is corn kernels that have been processed to remove the hull and germ, then soaked in lime, resulting in kernels with a soft, chewy texture. Find hominy in cans or dried. When hominy is dried and ground, it is called hominy grits. Hominy is a must for making posole, a delicious Mexican soup.

Liquid smoke: Liquid smoke, also called hickory liquid smoke, is an intensely aromatic and smoky-flavored liquid that makes foods taste as if they've been laboriously smoked for hours. The liquid comes from smoldered hickory wood, extracted through condensation. Look for the small bottles in the barbecue sauce aisle.

Miso: Miso is a very thick, salty, fermented paste made from soybeans and sometimes grains. Used to season almost anything from soups and sauces to dressings and main dishes, the white—or light—miso has a mild salty flavor. Red miso is more intense in color and flavor because of longer fermentation. Buy it in Asian markets or natural food stores and store in the refrigerator.

Nutritional yeast flakes: Nutritional yeast enhances foods with a pleasant, delicate cheese-like flavor. This yeast is uniquely different from the yeast used to leaven bread and unrelated to brewer's yeast. Find it in the supplements section of natural food markets.

Pomegranate molasses: Pomegranate juice that's been carefully simmered over very low heat until most of the water has evaporated becomes the thickened and syrupy pomegranate molasses, also called pomegranate syrup or paste. Pomegranate molasses is used as a condiment and a flavoring.

Potato flour: Potato flour is made from potatoes that have been cooked, dried, and finely ground. It is often used in gluten-free baking and in Jewish cooking as an ideal thickener for soups, sauces, stews, and potato latkes.

Tahini: Tahini is a flavorful, creamy paste made from ground, hulled, raw or roasted sesame seeds. Tahini is one of the main flavoring ingredients in hummus, baba ganoush, and a traditional sauce served with falafel. Use it in salad dressings, sauces, and for flavoring fruit and nut confections.

Tapioca flour: Tapioca flour is a white, powdery, starchy flour made from the cassava plant, native to Brazil. It binds and thickens like nothing else. Because tapioca flour is gluten-free, it often replaces wheat flour in baked goods and makes an ideal binder for some desserts. Look for it in natural food markets.

Tomatillos: Tomatillos are little green tomatoes, about the size of plump cherry tomatoes, enclosed in thin, paper-like, brown husks. Tomatillos impart an exceptional lemony flavor to salads, soups, main dishes, and salsas. Keep them in their husks until you're ready to use them, then discard the husks and wash the tomatillos. Don't worry about the somewhat sticky surface even after washing—it's natural, too.

Index

flour, potato, 139
flour, tapioca, 139
Fruit Relish, Cranberry and Winter, 87
Fruit Stuffing, Savory Chestnut and, 32–33
Fry, Hanukkah Gelt Stir-, 88
Fry, Red Cabbage and Apple Stir-, 26

G

garbanzo beans (chickpeas), 137
Garlicky Chestnut Butter, 9
Garlicky Roasted Cauliflower, 65
Gelt Stir-Fry, Hanukkah, 88
ginger
    Cookies, Chewy, 136
    Cream, Sweet Potato Pie with Cashew-, 106
    Glazed Carrots, Orange-, 22
    and Mint, Pomegranate-Apple Salad with, 13
Glazed Beets in Maple-Balsamic Sauce, 64
Glazed Carrots, Orange-Ginger, 22
Glögg, Happy New Year, 131
Golden Squash Concerto, 23
Go Seoul Searching, Brussels Sprouts, 63
Goulash, Old World Vegetable, 80–81
gram flour (chickpea flour), 137
Grape and Pomegranate Punch, Hot Mulled, 74
Gravy, Mashed Potatoes with Onion-Chardonnay, 28–29
green beans, in stir-fry, 88
green bell pepper(s)
    in chili
        Barn-Burner, 124–25
        Old-Fashioned, 128–29
        Sicilian, Two-Ways, 126–27
    in soup, 122
Green Christmas Tree, Jolly, 43
green olives, in chili, 126–27
Greens with Tempeh Bacon, Mustard, 104
green tomatoes (tomatillos), 139
Gremolata, New Year Log in Spicy Pecan, 116–17
Groundnut Stew, 97
guar gum, 138

H

Hanukkah, 75
    Borscht, Sweet and Sour Cabbage, 76–77
    Cholent, Mushroom-Barley, 78
    Coleslaw, Horseradish, 86
    Compote with Choco-Wafers, Pear and Walnut, 90–91
    Eggplant with Creamy Beet and Horseradish Sauce, 89
    Goulash, Old World Vegetable, 80–81
    Latkes, Beet, 83
    Latkes with Tofu Sour Cream and Applesauce, Potato, 82
    Raisin-Nut Cabbage Rolls with Sweet and Sour Sauce, 84–85
    Relish, Cranberry and Winter Fruit, 87
    Stir-Fry, Gelt, 88
    Strudel, Cranberry Apple, 92–93
    Tzimmes, Carrot and Sweet Potato, 79
Happy New Year Glögg, 131
harina de garbanzo (chickpea flour), 137
Harvest Succotash, 21
Hazelnut-Cranberry Bread Pudding with Crème Anglaise, 132–33
Hazelnut Sticky Pie, Apricot, Date, and, 134
Holiday Nog, Brandied, 130
Holiday-Ready Apple Crisp, 34
Holy Moly Posole, 58–59
Homemade Parmesan, 114
hominy, 138
Hoppin' John, 103
Horseradish Coleslaw, 86
Horseradish Sauce, Eggplant with Creamy Beet and, 89
Hot Mulled Grape and Pomegranate Punch, 74
Hot Spiced Cranberry Punch, 130
Hungarian goulash, 80–81

I

Indian succotash dish, 21

About the Author

WHEN ZEL ALLEN GOT MARRIED, SHE DIDN'T KNOW HOW TO COOK. But she acquired a husband with a daring and venturesome palate. As the kitchen adventures grew, so did Zel's cooking ability, eventually blossoming into a catering business.

When a focus on healthy eating opened a new door, the vegan journey led Zel to partner with her husband, Reuben, to publish *Vegetarians in Paradise*, an online vegetarian magazine read by more than 100,000 visitors monthly. Together, they write and edit articles that provide a wide range of resources for the vegan community. The publication spotlights Zel's humorous illustrations and her innovative recipes.

A medical study touting the health benefits of nuts sparked Zel's curiosity, and this new interest soon morphed into *The Nut Gourmet*, her nut-filled cookbook including everything from soup to, well, nuts!

Zel's interest in exotic foreign cuisines led to travel and food articles in *The Vegetarian Journal*.

Presently, Zel spreads the message of a healthy vegan lifestyle by teaching vegan cooking classes. She lives in suburban Los Angeles, with her husband and once homeless cat, Fuzzy.

Book Publishing Co.

books that educate, inspire, and empower

To find your favorite vegetarian and soyfood products online, visit:
www.healthy-eating.com

The Nut Gourmet
Zel Allen
978-1-57067-191-3
$19.95

Cooking Vegan
*Vesanto Melina, MS, RD,
and Joseph Forest*
978-1-57067-267-5
$19.95

The (Almost) No Fat
Holiday Cookbook
Bryanna Clark Grogan
978-1-57067-009-1
$12.95

Jazzy Vegetarian
Laura Theodore
978-1-57067-261-3
$24.95

The New Enlightened Eating
Caroline Marie Dupont
978-0-920470-83-1
$19.95

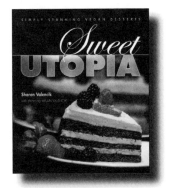

Sweet Utopia
Sharon Valencik
978-1-57067-233-0
$19.95

Purchase these health titles and cookbooks from your local bookstore or natural food store,
or you can buy them directly from:

Book Publishing Company • P.O. Box 99 • Summertown, TN 38483 • 1-800-695-2241

Please include $3.95 per book for shipping and handling.